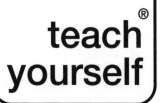

teach
yourself

instant japanese
elisabeth smith

language consultant:
helen gilhooly

For UK order enquiries: please contact Bookpoint Ltd, 130 Milton Park, Abingdon, Oxon, OX14 4SB. Telephone: +44 (0) 1235 827720. Fax: +44 (0) 1235 400454. Lines are open 09.00–17.00, Monday to Saturday, with a 24-hour message answering service. Details about our titles and how to order are available at www.teachyourself.co.uk

For USA order enquiries: please contact McGraw-Hill Customer Services, PO Box 545, Blacklick, OH 43004-0545, USA. Telephone: 1-800-722-4726. Fax: 1-614-755-5645.

For Canada order enquiries: please contact McGraw-Hill Ryerson Ltd, 300 Water St, Whitby, Ontario L1N 9B6, Canada. Telephone: 905 430 5000. Fax: 905 430 5020.

Long renowned as the authoritative source for self-guided learning – with more than 50 million copies sold worldwide – the **teach yourself** series includes over 500 titles in the fields of languages, crafts, hobbies, business, computing and education.

British Library Cataloguing in Publication Data: a catalogue record for this title is available from the British Library.

Library of Congress Catalog Card Number: on file.

First published in UK 2000 by Hodder Education, 338 Euston Road, London, NW1 3BH.

First published in US 2000 by The McGraw-Hill Companies, Inc.

2nd edition published 2003. 3rd edition published 2006.

The **teach yourself** name is a registered trade mark of Hodder Headline.

Copyright © 2000, 2003, 2006 Elisabeth Smith

Typeset by Transet Limited, Coventry, England.
Printed in Great Britain for Hodder Education, a division of Hodder Headline, 338 Euston Road, London, NW1 3BH, by Cox & Wyman Ltd, Reading, Berkshire.

The publisher has used its best endeavours to ensure that the URLs for external websites referred to in this book are correct and active at the time of going to press. However, the publisher and the author have no responsibility for the websites and can make no guarantee that a site will remain live or that the content will remain relevant, decent or appropriate.

Hodder Headline's policy is to use papers that are natural, renewable and recyclable products and made from wood grown in sustainable forests. The logging and manufacturing processes are expected to conform to the environmental regulations of the country of origin.

Impression number   10 9 8 7 6 5 4 3 2 1
Year   2010 2009 2008 2007 2006

contents

If, like me, you usually skip introductions, don't! Read on! You need to know how **Instant Japanese** works and why.

When I decided to write the **Instant** series I first called it *Barebones*, because that's what you want: *no frills, no fuss, just the bare bones and go!* So in **Instant Japanese** you'll find:

- Less than 500 words to say everything, well... nearly everything.

- No ghastly grammar – just a few useful tips.

- No time wasters such as 'the pen of my aunt...'

- No phrase book phrases for taking lessons in sumo wrestling.

- No need to be perfect. Mistakes won't spoil your success.

I've put some 30 years of teaching experience into this course. I know how people learn. I also know how long they are motivated by a new project (a few weeks) and how little time they can spare to study each day (under an hour). That's why you'll complete **Instant Japanese** in six weeks and get away with 45 minutes a day.

Of course there is some learning to do, but I have tried to make it as much fun as possible, even when it is boring. You'll meet Tom and Kate Walker on holiday in Japan. They do the kind of things you need to know about: shopping, eating out and getting about. As you will note, Tom and Kate speak **Instant Japanese** all the time, even to each other. What paragons of virtue!

To get the most out of this course, there are only two things you really should do:

- Follow the **Day-by-day guide** as suggested. Please don't skip bits and short-change your success. Everything is there for a reason.
- If you are a complete beginner, buy the recording that accompanies this book. It will help you to speak faster and with confidence.

When you have filled in your **Certificate** at the end of the book and can speak **Instant Japanese**, I would like to hear from you. Why not visit my website www.elisabeth-smith.co.uk, e-mail me at elisabeth.smith@hodder.co.uk, or write to me care of Hodder Education, 338 Euston Road, London, NW1 3BH?

Elisabeth Smith

The author would like to thank Helen Gilhooly, who acted as a language consultant in the preparation of this book.

how this book works

Instant Japanese has been structured for your rapid success. This is how it works:

Day-by-day guide Stick to it. If you miss a day, add one.

Dialogues Follow Tom and Kate through Japan. The English is in 'Japanese-speak' to get you tuned in.

New words Don't fight them, don't skip them – learn them! The flash cards will help you.

Good news grammar After you read it you can forget half and still succeed! That's why it's good news.

Flash words and flash sentences Read about these building blocks in the flash card section on page 92. Then use them!

Learn by heart Obligatory! Memorizing puts you on the fast track to speaking in full sentences.

Let's speak Japanese *You* will be doing the talking – in Japanese.

Spot the keys Listen to rapid Japanese and make sense of it.

Say it simply Learn how to use plain, **Instant Japanese** to say what you want to say. Don't be shy!

Test your progress Mark your own test and be amazed by the result.

Answers This is where you'll find the answers to the exercises.

▶ This icon asks you to switch on the recording.

Pronunciation If you don't know about it and don't have the recording go straight to page 16. You need to know about pronunciation before you can start Week 1.

Progress chart Enter your score each week and monitor your progress. Are you going for *very good* or *outstanding*?

Certificate It's on the last page. In six weeks it will have your name on it!

At the end of each week record your test score on the Progress chart below.

At the end of the course throw out your worst result – anybody can have a bad week – and add up your *five* best weekly scores. Divide the total by five to get your average score and overall course result.

Write your result – *outstanding, excellent, very good* or *good* – on your **Certificate** at the end of the book. If you scored more than 80% enlarge it and frame it!

Progress chart

90–100%							*outstanding*
80–89%							*excellent*
70–79%							*very good*
60–69%							*good*
Weeks	1	2	3	4	5	6	

Total of five best weeks =

divided by five =

Your final result _____ %

01

week one

Study for 45 minutes – or a little longer if you can!

Day zero

- Start with **Read this first.**
- Read **How this book works**.

Day one

- Read **In the aeroplane**.
- Listen to/Read **Hikōki de**.
- Listen to/Read the **New words**, then learn some of them.

Day two

- Repeat **Hikōki de** and the **New words**.
- Listen to/Read **Pronunciation**.
- Learn more **New words**.

Day three

- Learn all the **New words** until you know them well.
- Use the 22 **Flash words** and use them to help you.
- Read and learn the **Good news grammar**.

Day four

- Cut out and learn the **Flash sentences**.
- Listen to/Read **Learn by heart**.

Day five

- Listen to/Read **Let's speak Japanese**.
- Revise! Tomorrow you'll be testing your progress.

Day six

- Listen to/Read **Let's speak more Japanese** (optional).
- Listen to/Read **Let's speak Japanese – fast and fluently** (optional).
- Translate **Test your progress**.

Day seven is your day off!

In the aeroplane

Tom and Kate Walker are on their way to Japan. They are boarding flight JG 802 to Osaka via Tokyo and squeeze past Jun Suzuki who is sitting in their row. (The English is in 'Japanese-speak' to get you tuned in.)

Tom	Excuse me, our seats number 9a and 9b are.
Jun	Oh really? A moment (little wait) please.
Tom	How do you do? Tom and Kate Walker (we) are.
Jun	How do you do? Suzuki (I) am called.
Tom	Of the company Suzuki (you) are?
Jun	No, there are many Suzukis. I Jun Suzuki am.
Tom	We Osaka to go. (And you) Mr Suzuki?
Jun	Tokyo to I go. (But) I Kyoto from am.
Tom	Oh, really? I May in Kyoto to went. Very beautiful (it) is. Work through Kyoto to (I) went.
Jun	Your work what is it?
Tom	Computer it is. At Unilever I work.
Jun	(And you) Miss Kate? Your work what is it? Where do you work?
Kate	Travel agency at I worked but now Rover at I work. Travel agency than (more) interesting it is.
Jun	London from are you?
Kate	Yes, London from we are. Three years for Manchester in we were. And then one year for New York in we were. Now Birmingham in we are.
Jun	I Japan Bank at worked. Then ten years for Honda at I work.
Tom	Honda how is it? Interesting is it?
Jun	Boring it is. Every day late until I work. But house and BMW I have. And wife and four children there are. Wife America from came. Los Angeles in parents are. Florida in friend is. Always America to (she) phones. Expensive it is!
Kate	Now (from) work on holiday we are. (You) Mr Suzuki, too?
Jun	No, May in holiday we have. Hokkaido to (we) go. There apartment (we) have. Phone there is not! Mobile phone (we) won't take.

▶ Hikōki de

Tom and Kate Walker are on their way to Japan. They are boarding flight JG 802 to Osaka via Tokyo and squeeze past Jun Suzuki who is sitting in their row.

Tom	Sumimasen, watashitachi no seki wa kyū ban no A to B des(u).
Jun	Aa, sō des(u) ka. Chotto matte kudasai.
Tom	Hajimemash(i)te. Tom to Kate Walker des(u).
Jun	Hajimemash(i)te. Suzuki des(u).
Tom	Kaisha no Suzuki des(u) ka.
Jun	Iie, Suzuki wa ooi des(u). Watashi wa Suzuki Jun des(u).
Tom	Watashitachi wa Ōsaka ni ikimas(u). Suzuki-san wa?
Jun	Tōkyō ni ikimas(u). Watashi wa Kyōto kara des(u).
Tom	Sō des(u) ka. Watashi wa go-gatsu ni Kyōto ni ikimash(i)ta. Totemo kirei des(u) ne. Shigoto de Kyōto ni ikimash(i)ta.
Jun	O-shigoto wa nan des(u) ka.
Tom	Konpyūta des(u). Unilever de hataraiteimas(u).
Jun	Kate-san wa? O-shigoto wa nan des(u) ka. Doko de hataraiteimas(u) ka.
Kate	Ryokō gaisha de hataraiteimash(i)ta ga ima Rover de hataraiteimas(u). Ryokō gaisha yori omoshiroi des(u).
Jun	London kara des(u) ka.
Kate	Hai, London kara des(u). San nenkan Manchester ni imash(i)ta. Sorekara ichi nenkan New York ni imash(i)ta. Ima Birmingham ni imas(u).
Jun	Watashi wa Nihon ginkō de hataraiteimash(i)ta. Sorekara jū nenkan Honda de hataraiteimas(u).
Tom	Honda wa dō des(u) ka. Omoshiroi des(u) ka.
Jun	Tsumaranai des(u). Mainichi osoku made hataraiteimas(u). Demo ie to BMW ga arimas(u). Sorekara tsuma to yonin no kodomo ga imas(u). Tsuma wa America kara kimash(i)ta. Los Angeles ni ryōshin ga imas(u). Florida ni tomodachi ga imas(u). Itsumo America ni denwa shiteimas(u). Takai des(u)!
Kate	Ima shigoto ga yasumi des(u). Suzuki-san mo?
Jun	Iie, go-gatsu ni yasumi ga arimas(u). Hokkaidō ni ikimas(u). Soko ni wa apāto ga arimas(u). Denwa ga arimasen! Keitai denwa o motteikimasen!

▶ New words

Cover up the Japanese words, then say them OUT LOUD.

sumimasen   *excuse me, sorry*
watashitachi   *we*
no   *of, from, 's (belonging to)*
watashitachi no   *our*
seki   *seat*
wa   *emphasizes the preceding word*
kyū   *nine*
ban   *number*
to   *and; with*
des(u)   *am, are, is*
aa, sō des(u) ka   *oh, really?/is that right? (lit. oh, is so?)*
ka   *tells you that sentence is a question*
chotto   *a little*
matte   *wait*
kudasai   *please (may I have?)*
hajimemash(i)te   *how do you do?*
kaisha   *company*
iie   *no*
ooi   *many*
ikimas(u)   *go, goes, is going, are going*
ni; de   *to, at, for, from, in*
-san   *Mr, Mrs, Ms (polite address)*
kara   *from*
watashi   *I*
go-gatsu   *May*
ikimash(i)ta   *went*
totemo   *very*
kirei(na)   *beautiful, pretty*
ne   *isn't it?*
shigoto, o-shigoto   *work, your work (polite)*
de   *through, by, within, on*
nan, nani   *what*
konpyūta   *computer*

hataraiteimas(u)   *work, works, am/are/is working*
doko   *where*
ryokō gaisha   *travel agency*
hataraiteimash(i)ta   *worked, was/were working*
ima   *now*
yori   *than*
motto   *more*
omoshiroi   *interesting*
hai   *yes*
san   *three*
nen/nenkan   *year/for the year*
imash(i)ta   *(we) were*
sorekara   *and, and then, after that*
ichi   *one*
Nihon ginkō   *Bank of Japan*
jū   *ten*
dō   *how, what*
tsumaranai   *boring*
mainichi   *every day*
osoku   *late*
made   *until, to*
demo   *but, however*
ie   *house*
(ga) arimas(u)   *have (own); is*
tsuma   *(your own) wife*
yon, yonin   *four, four people*
kodomo   *children*
(ga) imas(u)   *is, there is (for people and animals)*
kimash(i)ta   *(she) came*
ryōshin   *parents*
tomodachi   *friend*
itsumo   *always*
denwa   *telephone, tel. call*
denwa shiteimas(u)   *(she) telephones*
takai   *expensive, high*

yasumi *holiday*	**arimasen** *am not, are not, is not (talking about things)*
mo *also*	
soko *there*	**keitai denwa** *mobile phone*
apāto *apartment*	**motteikimasen** *won't/don't take*

> **TOTAL NEW WORDS: 75**
> **…only 313 words to go!**

Some easy extras

Numbers 1–12

zero/rei	ichi	ni	san	shi/yon	go	roku
0	1	2	3	4	5	6

shichi/nana	hachi	kyū/ku	jū	jūichi	jūni
7	8	9	10	11	12

The months

These are very easy in Japanese.

The numbers 1–12 will indicate the month: 1 is January, 2 is February and so on.

All you need to know is the word for month: *gatsu*. You add this to the number and you have the name of the month: *January*: **ichi-gatsu**, *February*: **ni-gatsu**... easy!

Some more greetings

Ohayō gozaimasu *good morning*, **konnichiwa** *hello, good afternoon*, **konbanwa** *good evening*, **oyasumi nasai** *good night*, **sayōnara** *goodbye*, **ja mata ne** *see you!*

▶ Pronunciation

To pronounce Japanese is not difficult – especially if you buy the recording to hear the 'real thing'.

As you can see, the Japanese in this book has been transliterated, i.e. changed from Japanese script into European style writing. This makes it quite easy to read and pronounce.

There are five vowels

The word in brackets gives you an example of the sound. Say the word OUT LOUD and then the Japanese example OUT LOUD.

a	(*America*)	kara
e	(*yes*)	demo
i	(*field*)	ima
o	(*not*)	chotto
u	(*June*)	tsuma

Always say each vowel separately but smoothly. So **kaisha** would not be pronounced 'kaysha' but **ka–i–sha**. And **kirei** is pronounced **ki-re-i**. Doubles like **iie** or **ooi** are all said separately: **i-i-e** and **o-o-i**.

Consonants

Pronounce them just like in English but watch out for these:

ch	like in	*child*	(not like in *charisma*)
f			is quite soft. Try to say it without your teeth touching your lips.
g	like in	**g**o	(not like in *Gillian*)
j	like in	*jam*	(not like in the German *ja*)
tt			when you come across any doubles, pause a little before you say them. So it's **ma-tte**, not **matte**.
ya, yo, yu			Each makes just one sound. So it's **Kyō–to** not **Ky-yo-to**.

When you find a line over a vowel, it is a long one – hold it twice as long as you would normally. So **Tōkyō** would be **Toh –kyoh**.

When you first hear Japanese it may sound strangely 'flat'. This is because all syllables are given the same amount of stress. Many English people pronounce Hiroshima like this: Hiro**shi**ma or Hiro**shi**ma. It should be: Hi-ro-shi-ma, giving equal stress to each syllable.

Attention! The **-u** and the **-i** are almost silent in 'desu' and words ending '-masu', '-mashita', and '-mashite'. To remind you, in Week 1 **-u** and **-i** appear in brackets in these words.

▶ Good news grammar

This is the **Good news** part of each lesson. No ghastly grammar – just a few explanations on the difference between English and Japanese – to get you to speak Japanese **Instantly!**

1 Word order...

...or getting used to things being 'back to front'. When you want to say *I am going to Tokyo. I am from Kyoto*, you have to think... 'Tokyo to I am going': **Tōkyō ni ikimas(u)** and 'Kyoto from I am': **Kyōto kara des(u)**. As you can see, the preposition – *to, at, in, from* etc. – goes *after* the place, and the verb goes to the end. So, practise talking backwards!

2 'The' and 'a'

The Japanese don't use an article. So it's not *the bank*, but quite simply *bank*. *I worked at (the) bank*: **Ginkō de hataraiteimash(i)ta**.

3 Asking a question

That's easy! Just add **ka** at the end. No need for a question mark. *Are you from London?*... 'London from you are?'... **London kara des(u) ka**.

4 Des(u)

This can mean: *I am, you are, he/she/it is, we are, you are, they are*. Wow! One word, **des(u)**, for all that? So how do you know which one it is? Well, usually the meaning of the sentence will tell you. Relax! But if you want to make it quite clear who is talking you can say **watashi**: *I*, or **watashitachi**: *we*.

5 Wa

This seems to be popping up all over the place, 13 times in the dialogue alone! When you spot it look left! The word before **wa** tells you what this sentence is about. The **wa** simply alerts you to it (backwards of course!). Here's an example from the dialogue: **Honda wa dō des(u) ka**. *How is Honda*? The **wa** makes it quite clear that Honda is the main topic of this sentence. Overkill? No, you know where you stand!

6 Addressing people

The Japanese are very polite. When they address you they will usually not say *you* but repeat your name, adding –**san**: *You, (Kate)*... **Kate-san**.

With certain words an **o–** is put in front. This makes them more respectful. This can sometimes be translated as *your* e.g. **shigoto**, *work*; **o-shigoto**, *your work*. Sounds rather smart, doesn't it?

7 Bits and bobs

In the texts and exercises you will come across some little words like **wa, ga, o, no** or **ni** that pop up when you don't expect or can't explain them. In **Instant Japanese** you are allowed to ignore them.

▶ Learn by heart

Don't be tempted to skip this exercise because it reminds you of school... If you want to **speak**, not stumble, saying a few lines by heart does the trick. Learn **...Des(u)** by heart after you have filled in the gaps with your personal, or any, information.

Example   **Brian Smith des(u).**
                     Birmingham kara des(u).

When you know the eight lines by heart go over them again until you can say them aloud fluently and fairly fast. Can you beat 40 seconds? Excellent!

...Des(u)

.........................**(first name)**.........................**(surname)** des(u).

.........................**(place)** kara des(u).

.........................**(place)** ni go-gatsu ni imash(i)ta.

San nenkan.........**(name of company)** de hataraiteimash(i)ta.

Ima.....................**(name of company)** de hataraiteimas(u).

.........................**(place)** ni ie ga arimas(u). Kirei des(u).

Roku-gatsu ni.........................**(place)** ni ikimas(u).

Tōkyō wa dō des(u) ka.

▶ Let's speak Japanese

If you have the recording, listen to check your answers to **Let's speak Japanese**.

Here are ten English sentences. Read each sentence and say it in Japanese – OUT LOUD.

1 My name is Tom Walker.
2 Are you from London?
3 No, I am from Manchester.
4 I have an apartment in Tokyo.
5 I do not have a house.

6 We work at Honda.
7 The work is interesting.
8 Where do you go in May?
9 Where is your company?
10 Japan is a little expensive.

Well, how many did you tick? If you are not happy, do it again! Now here are some questions in Japanese, and you are going to answer in Japanese. Answer all questions starting with **hai**.

11 Ōsaka kara des(u) ka.
12 Honda de hataraiteimas(u) ka.
13 Kodomo ga imas(u) ka.
14 Apāto wa takai des(u) ka.
15 Tōkyō ni ikimas(u) ka.
16 Tom Walker-san des(u) ka.
17 BMW ga arimas(u) ka.
18 Konpyūta wa takai des(u) ka.
19 America de hataraiteimas(u) ka.
20 Ōsaka wa omoshiroi des(u) ka.

Answers

1 Tom Walker des(u).
2 London kara des(u) ka.
3 Iie, Manchester kara des(u).
4 Tōkyō ni apāto ga arimas(u).
5 Ie ga arimasen.
6 Honda de hataraiteimas(u).
7 Shigoto wa omoshiroi des(u).
8 Go-gatsu ni doko ni ikimas(u) ka.
9 Kaisha wa doko ni arimas(u) ka/ doko des(u) ka.
10 Nihon wa chotto takai des(u).

11 Hai, Ōsaka kara des(u).
12 Hai, Honda de hataraiteimas(u).
13 Hai, kodomo ga imas(u).
14 Hai, apāto wa takai des(u).
15 Hai, Tōkyō ni ikimas(u).
16 Hai, Tom Walker des(u).
17 Hai, BMW ga arimas(u).
18 Hai, konpyūta wa takai des(u).
19 Hai, America de hataraiteimas(u).
20 Hai, Ōsaka wa omoshiroi des(u).

Well, what was your score? If you got 20 ticks you can give yourself 3 gold stars!

▶ Let's speak more Japanese

Here are some optional exercises. They may stretch the 45 minutes a day by 15 minutes. But the extra practice will be worth it.

And always remember: near enough is good enough!

In your own words

This exercise will teach you to express yourself freely. Use only the words you have learned so far.

Tell me in your own words that...

1 you originate from Manchester
2 you have an American friend
3 you have to work long hours
4 but you have a house and a Rolls-Royce
5 you have four children
6 your wife comes from Tokyo
7 you work at a travel agency; it's boring
8 your wife works for the Japan Bank
9 you own a property in Florida
10 you have a vacation in April (**shi-gatsu**)

Answers

1 Manchester kara des(u).
2 Tomodachi wa Amerika kara des(u).
3 Mainichi osoku made hataraiteimas(u).
4 Demo ie to Rolls-Royce ga arimas(u).
5 Yonin no kodomo ga imas(u).
6 Tsuma wa Tokyo kara kimash(i)ta.
7 Ryokō gaisha de hataraiteimas(u). Tsumaranai des(u).
8 Tsuma wa Nihon ginkō de hataraiteimas(u).
9 Florida ni apāto ga arimas(u).
10 Shi-gatsu ni yasumi ga arimas(u).

▶ Let's speak Japanese – fast and fluently

No more stuttering and stumbling! Get out the stopwatch and time yourself with this fluency practice.

Translate each section and check if it is correct. Then cover the answers and say the three or four sentences fast!

20 seconds per section for a silver star, 15 seconds for a gold star.

Some of the English is in 'Japanese-speak' to help you.

Good Evening. I Tokyo to go. (And you), Mr Suzuki?
I Osaka bank at, work. Now Kyoto to go.
Holidays (I) have – computer (I) have not!

Konbanwa. Watashi wa Tokyo ni ikimas(u). Suzuki-san wa?
Watashi wa Ōsaka ginkō de hataraiteimas(u). Ima Kyōto ni ikimas(u).
Yasumi ga arimas(u) – Konpyūta ga arimasen!

Kyoto how is it? Interesting is it?
Interesting it is but expensive it is.
There apartment (I) have.
Wife there is, Michiko.

Kyōto wa dō des(u) ka. Omoshiroi des(u) ka.
Omoshiroi des(u) ga takai des(u).
Soko ni wa apāto ga arimas(u).
Tsuma ga imas(u), Michiko-san.

New York in (her) friend is.
Always America to (she) phones.
Expensive it is!
Oh, excuse me, it is Michiko. One moment, please.
(She) always speaking on the phone.

New York ni tomodachi ga imas(u).
Itsumo Amerika ni denwa shiteimas(u).
Takai des(u)!
Aa, sumimasen, Michiko-san des(u). Chotto matte kudasai.
Itsumo denwa shiteimas(u).

Now say all the sentences in Japanese without stopping and starting. If you can do it in under one minute you are a fast and fluent winner!

But if you are not happy with your result – just try once more.

Test your progress

This is your only written exercise. You'll be amazed how easy it is!

Translate the 15 sentences without looking at the previous pages.

1 Mr Suzuki, how do you do?
2 Japan is very interesting.
3 Where is the house?
4 I have an apartment in London.
5 We have three children (**Sannin no kodomo**).
6 London is beautiful in June.
7 Excuse me, where is a travel agent?
8 We have a friend at the bank.
9 Are you working every day?
10 I always go to Hong Kong.
11 My wife worked in America until January.
12 I also went to Hokkaido.
13 How is Jun's BMW?
14 Are you going to the apartment?
15 I work until late. It is boring.

When you have finished all 15 sentences look up the answers on page 86, and mark your work. Then enter your result on the Progress chart on page 9. If your score is higher than 80% you'll have done very well indeed!

02

week two

Forty-five minutes a day – but a little extra will step up your progress!

Day one

- Read **In Kyōto**.
- Listen to/Read **Kyōto de**.
- Listen to/Read the **New words**. Learn 20 easy ones.

Day two

- Repeat **Kyōto de** and the **New words**.
- Go over **Pronunciation**.
- Learn the harder **New words**.
- Use the **Flash words** to help you.

Day three

- Learn all the **New words** until you know them well.
- Read and learn the **Good news grammar**.

Day four

- Cut out and learn the **Flash sentences**.
- Listen to/Read **Learn by heart**.

Day five

- Listen to/Read **Let's speak Japanese**.
- Go over **Learn by heart**.

Day six

- Listen to/Read **Let's speak more Japanese** (optional).
- Listen to/Read **Let's speak Japanese – fast and fluently** (optional).
- Translate **Test your progress**.

Day seven is a study-free day!

day-by-day guide

In Kyoto

On arrival in Kyoto, Tom and Kate go to the tourist office to find somewhere to stay. They are given the name and address of Mrs Fumi Yamaguchi. Later they go to a coffee shop and speak to Kengo, the waiter... (The English is in 'Japanese-speak' to get you tuned in.)

Kate   Hello. We Kate and Tom Walker are. One night we want (but) not very expensive double room do you have?

Fumi   Yes, Japanese-style room we have. Japanese bath also there is.

Tom   Really? How much is it?

Fumi   For two people 7,000 yen it is but credit cards we don't use.

Kate   OK, one night please.

Fumi   This way please. Left side it is. Not very big it is but...

Kate   A bit small it is but very nice room it is.

Fumi   Breakfast is 8 o'clock from, 10 o'clock half past until.

Kate   7 o'clock 45 minutes at, breakfast we want to eat. 8 o'clock 15 minutes at, Nara to we want to go, that is the reason.

Fumi   Certainly.

Kate   Excuse me, coffee we want to drink. Near here coffee shop is there?

Fumi   Yes, there is. Here from, five minutes it is. Thirty metres go then right turn and then straight ahead go please.

(In the coffee shop)

Kate   Coffee and black tea may we have.

Kengo   Sandwiches, toast, cake and so on also we have (but)...

Tom   OK, toast two may we have... this table a bit dirty isn't it?

Kate   But the toilets clean aren't they?

Tom   This black tea not very hot is.

Kate   But this coffee shop not bad is it?

Tom   This toast not delicious is.

Kate   But that waiter very handsome is, isn't he?

Tom   What! (*to the waiter*) Excuse me, altogether how much is it?

Kengo   Two thousand yen it is.

▶ Kyōto de

On arrival in Kyoto, Tom and Kate go to the tourist office to find somewhere to stay. They are given the name and address of Mrs Fumi Yamaguchi. Later they go to a coffee shop and speak to Kengo, the waiter...

Kate	Konnichiwa. Watashitachi wa Kate to Tom Walker desu. Ippaku shitai desu ga amari takakunai daburu no heya ga arimasu ka.
Fumi	Hai, washitsu ga arimasu. Ofuro mo arimasu.
Tom	Sō desu ka. Ikura desu ka.
Fumi	Futari de nana-sen en desu ga kurejitto kādo wa tsukaemasen.
Kate	Ja, ippaku onegaishimasu.
Fumi	Kochira e dōzo. Hidarigawa ni arimasu. Amari hirokunai n desu ga...
Kate	Chotto semai desu ga totemo ii heya desu.
Fumi	Asagohan wa hachi ji kara jū ji han made desu.
Kate	Shichi ji yonjūgo-hun sugi ni asagohan o tabetai desu. Hachi ji jūgo-hun sugi ni Nara ni ikitai desu kara.
Fumi	Kashikomarimashita.
Kate	Sumimasen, kōhī o nomitai desu. Kono chikaku ni kissaten ga arimasu ka.
Fumi	Hai, arimasu. Koko kara go-fun desu. Sanjū mētoru itte, migi ni magatte, massugu itte kudasai.
(In the coffee shop)	
Kate	Kōhī to kōcha o kudasai.
Kengo	Sandoicchi, tōsuto, kēki nado mo arimasu ga...
Tom	Ja, tōsuto o futatsu kudasai... kono tēburu wa chotto kitanai desu ne.
Kate	Demo toire wa kirei desu ne.
Tom	Kono kōcha wa amari atsukunai desu.
Kate	Demo kono kissaten wa warukunai desu ne.
Tom	Kono tōsuto wa oishikunai desu.
Kate	Demo ano uētā wa totemo hansamu desu ne.
Tom	Ē! *(to the waiter)* Sumimasen, zembu de ikura desu ka.
Kengo	Nisen en desu.

▶ New words

Learning words the traditional way can be boring. If you enjoyed the flash cards, why not make your own for the rest of the words? Always remember to say the words OUT LOUD. It's the fast track to speaking!

ippaku   *one night*
shitai desu   *I, we, etc. want to do*
amari   *not very*
takakunai   *not expensive*
daburu   *double*
heya   *room*
washitsu   *Japanese-style room*
ofuro   *Japanese bath*
ikura   *how much?*
futari de   *for two, for a couple*
nana-sen en   *7,000 yen*
   (sen = 1,000, en = yen)
kurejitto kādo   *credit card*
tsukaemasen   *can't use*
ja   *right*
onegaishimasu   *please*
kochira   *this way*
dōzo   *go ahead/here you are*
hidarigawa   *left side*
hirokunai   *not spacious*
n desu   *(when stating a fact)*
ga   *but...*
semai   *small, narrow*
ii   *good, nice, all right*
asagohan   *breakfast*
hachi ji   *8 o'clock*
ashita   *tomorrow*
jū ji han   *10.30*
shichi ji yonjūgo-fun   *quarter to eight*
tabetai desu   *want to eat*
jūgo-hun sugi   *15 minutes, quarter past*

ikitai desu   *want to go*
kara   *(used when giving reason)*
kashikomarimashita   *certainly*
kōhī   *coffee*
nomitai desu   *want to drink*
kono chikaku ni   *near here*
kissaten   *coffee shop*
koko   *this place, here*
go-hun sugi   *five minutes past*
sanjū mētoru   *30 m*
itte   *go and then...*
migi   *right*
magatte   *turn and then*
massugu   *straight on*
kōcha   *black tea*
sandoicchi   *sandwiches*
tōsuto   *toast*
kēki   *cake*
nado   *etc.*
futatsu   *two items*
kono   *this*
tēburu   *table*
kitanai   *dirty*
toire   *toilets*
atsukunai   *not hot*
warukunai   *not bad*
oishikunai   *not delicious*
ano   *that*
uētā   *waiter*
hansamu   *handsome*
Ē   *What!*
zembu de   *altogether*

TOTAL NEW WORDS: 62
...only 251 words to go!

Some useful extras

More numbers

13 **jūsan** (10 + 3)	14 **jūshi/jūyon**	15 **jūgo**	16 **jūroku**
17 **jūshichi/jūnana**	18 **jūhachi**	19 **jūkyu/jūku**	20 **nijū**
21 **nijūichi**	22 **nijūni**	30 **sanjū**	40 **yonjū**
50 **gojū**	60 **rokujū**	70 **nanajū**	80 **hachijū**
90 **kyūjū**	100 **hyaku**	1,000 **sen**	
10,000 **man**	20,000 **niman**		

▶ Good news grammar

1 Want to: *tai desu*

To say: *I want to, you want to* or *we want to... do something* you replace **masu** with **tai desu**.

So when Kate says: *we want to eat* or *we want to go*

tabemasu *we eat* becomes **tabetai desu** *we want to eat* and **ikimasu** *we go* becomes **ikitai desu** *we want to go*.

Now look through the dialogue for the rest of the **tai desu**. Did you find **shitai desu** and **nomitai desu**? Tai desu: *easy enough*.

2 *Kunai*: saying 'not'

When you describe something saying that it is not big or not expensive you do a little 'surgery and hip replacement': you cut off the last letter from the adjective and replace it with **kunai**.

So, **hiroi** *big* becomes **hirokunai** *not big*, and **takai** *expensive* becomes **takakunai** *not expensive*.

Some adjectives, like **kirei** *beautiful* and **hansamu** *handsome*, do their own thing. But don't worry about them.

If you want to add 'very' use **totemo** for the positive and **amari** for the negative. *The room is not very big but very nice*: **Amari hirokunai n desu ga... totemo ii heya desu.**

3 *Ni*: on, at, to. Remember to look left!

When you spot **ni** look left, at the previous word. Then read backwards:

Example hidarigawa *the left side*, hidarigawa ni *on the left side*

4 Telling the time: easy!

To say: *o'clock* is easy. Say the number and add ...**ji**.

Example **hachi ji** *eight o'clock*.

To say *past*, like in *five minutes past* or *quarter past*, is easy too: just add **hun sugi** *minute* to the number.

Example *five past*: **go-hun sugi**, *quarter past (15 minutes)*: **jūgo-hun sugi**, *quarter to (45 minutes past)*: **yonjūgo-hun sugi**

Sometimes **hun** turns to **pun** or **bun**, like in *ten past*: **juppun sugi**. It just sounds better.

Here are some bonus times:
asa: *morning*   **kesa**: *this morning*
gogo: *afternoon, p.m.*   **ashita**: *tomorrow*
ban/yoru: *evening*   **konban**: *this evening*
What time is it? **Nan ji desu ka.**
(At) what time is...? **...wa nan ji desu ka.**
It is at...o'clock **...ji desu**
four o'clock **yo ji**
nine o'clock **ku ji**
half past **han**; *half past nine* **ku ji han**

▶ Learn by heart

Learn the following seven lines by heart. Try to say them in under one minute and with a bit of drama. You'll remember them better that way.

> **Kono chikaku ni ii kissaten ga arimasu...**
> Kono chikaku ni ii kissaten ga arimasu.
> Kurejitto kādo wa tsukaemasen ga amari takakunai desu.
> Sandoicchi, kōhī nado ga arimasu.
> Soshite asagohan wa shichi ji kara jūichi ji made desu.
> Asagohan wa futari de sen en dake desu.
> Kōcha wa amari atsukunai desu ga toire wa kirei desu.
> Soshite* uētā wa totemo hansamu desu!

*and

▶ Let's speak Japanese

Over to you! I'll give you ten English sentences and you say them in Japanese OUT LOUD! If you don't have the recording, check your answers against those printed below – but cover them up so that you can see only one at a time. Unless you get eight out of ten, do the exercise again.

1 Do you have a double room?
2 Excuse me, how much is it?
3 What time is breakfast from?
4 Do you have a Japanese-style room?
5 One night please. (Please could we stay for one night?)
6 We want to drink some coffee.
7 Is there a coffee shop near here?
8 Is it on the left side or is it on the right side (use two sentences)?
9 May I have tea and a sandwich, please.
10 I work from nine o'clock to six o'clock.

Now answer these questions. Use **hai** where you can:

11 Heya wa amari takakunai desu ka.
12 Heya wa ikura desu ka.
13 Ofuro mo arimasu ka.
14 Kono chikaku ni kōshū (*public*) denwa ga arimasu ka.

Answer these questions with **iie**. Use **arimasen** (*there isn't/I haven't*) and replace **ga** with **wa**.

15 Kurejitto kādo ga arimasu ka.
16 Tōsuto ga arimasu ka.
17 Apāto ga arimasu ka.

Now think up your own answers. Yours might be different from mine but still be correct.

18 Doko ni ikimasu ka.
19 O-shigoto wa nan ji kara nan ji made desu ka.
20 Nihon no (*Japan's*) kissaten wa takai desu ka.

Answers

1 Daburu no heya ga arimasu ka.
2 Sumimasen, ikura desu ka.
3 Asagohan wa nan ji kara desu ka.
4 Washitsu ga arimasu ka.
5 Ippaku onegaishimasu.
6 Kōhī o nomitai desu.
7 Kono chikaku ni kissaten ga arimasu ka.
8 Hidarigawa ni arimasu ka. Migigawa ni arimasu ka.
9 Kōcha to sandoicchi o kudasai.
10 Ku ji kara roku ji made hataraiteimasu.

11 Hai, amari takakunai desu.
12 Futari de nana-sen en desu.
13 Hai, ofuro mo arimasu. (Or: hai, arimasu).
14 Hai, arimasu.
15 Iie, kurejitto kādo wa arimasen.
16 Iie, tōsuto wa arimasen.
17 Iie, apāto wa arimasen.
18 Kyōto ni ikimasu.
19 Shigoto wa ku ji kara go ji made desu.
20 Hai, totemo takai desu.

◘ Let's speak more Japanese

Here are the two optional exercises. Remember, they may stretch the 45 minutes a day by 15 minutes. But the extra practice will be worth it.

If you managed to get more than half right the first time, give yourself a double gold star!

In your own words

This exercise will teach you to express yourself freely. Use only the words you have learned so far.

Ask me in your own words...

1 if there is availability of a double room
2 what the price is for the room for one night
3 where you can have a coffee
4 if the café is straight ahead and on the left or on the right.

Tell me...

5 you would like breakfast at 7.30
6 you are thinking of going to Nara the next day
7 you want coffee and toast
8 what you don't like about the café (two sentences minimum)
9 what Kate says about the café. (Kate says: Kate-san wa... to iimasu)
10 that the bill is 3,000 yen altogether

Answers

1 (Sumimasen) Daburu no heya ga arimasu ka.
2 Ippaku ikura desu ka.
3 Kono chikaku ni kissaten ga arimasu ka.
4 Kissaten wa massugu desu ka. Hidarigawa desu ka. Migigawa desu ka (or you can use **ni arimasu ka** *is located* instead of **desu ka**).
5 Shichi ji han ni asagohan o tabetai desu.
6 Ashita Nara ni ikitai desu.
7 Kōhī to tōsuto o kudasai.
8 Kono tēburu wa chotto kitanai desu. Kono tōsuto wa oishikunai desu... (you may have had other opinions).
9 Kate-san wa 'Demo toire wa kirei desu ne. Ano uētā wa totemo hansamu desu ne' to iimasu.
10 Zembu de sanzen-en desu.

▶ Let's speak Japanese – fast and fluently

No more stuttering and stumbling! Get out the stopwatch and time yourself with this fluency practice.

Translate each section and check if it is correct. Then cover the answers and say the three or four sentences fast!

20 seconds per section for a silver star, 15 seconds for a gold star.

Some of the English is in 'Japanese-speak' to help you.

Good evening, Japanese-style room do you have? A bath also is there?
8,000 yen a little expensive is.
One night I would like.
The breakfast how much is it?

Konbanwa. Washitsu ga arimasu ka. Ofuro mo arimasu ka.
Hassen-en wa chotto takai desu.
Ippaku shitai desu.
Asagohan wa ikura desu ka?

My company is here near. Straight ahead it is. On the left it is.
But tomorrow to Osaka (I) am going.
11.30 at (I) would like to go.

Watashi no kaisha wa kono chikaku ni arimasu. Massugu desu.
Hidarigawa desu
(or you can use **ni arimasu** *is located* instead of **desu**).
Demo ashita Ōsaka ni ikimasu.
Jū ichi ji ni ikitai desu.

This café very small is. And (**So-shi-te**) expensive is.
The toilets dirty are.
The coffee is cold. And (**So-shi-te**) there is no tea.
How much is it? Two coffees are 2,000 yen!

Kono kissaten wa totemo semai desu. Soshite takai desu.
Toire wa kitanai desu.
Kōhī wa atsukunai desu. Soshite kōcha ga arimasen!
*Ikura desu ka. Futatsu no kōhī wa (or **kōhī wa futatsu**) nisen-en desu!*

Now say all the sentences in Japanese without stopping and starting. If you can do it in under a minute you are a fast and fluent winner!

But if you are not happy with your result – just try once more.

Test your progress

Translate these sentences into Japanese and write them out. See what you can remember without looking at the previous pages.

1 Could we have a coffee please?
2 Is there a bank near here?
3 We also have sandwiches, cakes and so on.
4 How much is the tea?
5 This cake is not very delicious.
6 What time is your work from?
7 They always go to the coffee shop at half past six.
8 Where are the toilets? Are they straight ahead?
9 Are you going to Hokkaido?
10 I went to Tokyo through work.
11 This breakfast is delicious. How much is it?
12 Where are you tomorrow at half past ten?
13 We don't take credit cards.
14 I am going to the travel agent's. And then (*after that* **sorekara**) I am going to America.
15 Excuse me, there is only the two of us.
16 All right, (we'll stay for) three nights (**sanpaku**) please.
17 The apartment is very big but a little expensive.
18 This room isn't bad, is it?
19 This not very hot tea is 700 yen.
20 The coffee shop is ten minutes from here.

Check your answers with the key on page 87 and work out your score. If it is above 70% you have done very well.

Now enter your result on the Progress chart in the front of the book.

03

week three

Study for 45 minutes a day – but there are no penalties for doing more!

Day one

- Read **Let's go shopping**.
- Listen to/Read **Kaimono o shimashō**.
- Listen to/Read the **New words**, then learn some of them.

Day two

- Repeat **Kaimono o shimashō** and the **New words**.
- Learn all the **New words**. Use the **Flash cards**!

Day three

- Test yourself on all the **New words** – boring, boring, but you are over halfway already!
- Listen to/Read **Learn by heart**.
- Read and learn the **Good news grammar**.

Day four

- Go over the **Good news grammar**.
- Cut out and learn the ten **Flash sentences**.

Day five

- Listen to/Read **Let's speak Japanese**.
- Listen to/Read **Spot the keys**.

Day six

- Go over **Learn by heart**.
- Have a quick look at **New words**, Weeks 1–3. You now know over 200 words! Well, more or less.
- Listen to/Read **Let's speak more Japanese** (optional).
- Listen to/Read **Let's speak Japanese – fast and fluently** (optional).
- Translate **Test your progress**.

Day seven – enjoy your day off!

day-by-day guide

Let's go shopping

Tom and Kate are now at a hotel in Nara. Kate plans some shopping, but Tom has other plans... (The English is in 'Japanese-speak' to get you tuned in.)

Kate Well, today shopping let's do/go. To the shopping centre shall we go?

Tom But the weather bad is. Cold it is. Television on, both football and tennis there is. And 12 half past at, golf there is.

Kate I'm sorry but bank to must go. And post office at, stamps buy and then chemist's and dry cleaner's to want to go.

Tom Right, golf is out. The football three o'clock from isn't it. Is that all?

Kate No, suitcase also I want to buy. And souvenirs I want to buy. Kimono I want to buy.

Tom You're kidding! The shops what time until are they (open)?

Kate Seven o'clock until they are (open).

Tom OK, football also is out. 8.15 from tennis I watch.
(Later)

Kate A bit I bought too much! Fans and dolls and chopsticks and cotton kimonos...

Tom No problem. Yesterday, nothing bought. That black bag, inside, what is there? Is it mine?

Kate Hmm... souvenir shop to I went and this blue kimono I saw. Beautiful, don't you think? The shop assistant very kind and Tom Cruise resembled.

Tom Tom Cruise, who is he? The kimono how much was it?

Kate A bit expensive but Tokyo in it is very expensive you know!

Tom What! Have you gone crazy?

Kate But... this golf T-shirt was very cheap. Size 50 it is. And English newspaper I bought. Here you are ... now from television on, sumo (wrestling) is there?

▶ Kaimono o shimashō

Tom and Kate are now at a hotel in Nara. Kate plans some shopping, but Tom has other plans...

Kate Sā, kyō kaimono o shimashō. Shōtengai ni ikimashō ka.

Tom Demo tenki ga warui desu. Samui desu. Terebi de sakkā mo tenisu mo arimasu. Sorekara jūni ji han ni gorufu ga arimasu.

Kate Mōshiwake arimasen ga ginkō ni ikanakereba narimasen. Soshite yūbinkyoku de kitte o katte, kusuriya to dorai kurīningu ni ikitai desu.

Tom Ja, gorufu wa dame desu. Sakkā wa san ji kara desu ne. Sore dake desu ka.

Kate Iie, sūtsukēsu mo kaitai desu. Soshite omiyage o kaitai desu. Kimono o kaitai desu.

Tom Uso! Mise wa nan ji made desu ka.

Kate Shichi ji made desu.

Tom Ja, sakkā mo dame desu. Demo hachi ji jūgo-hun sugi kara tenisu o mimasu.

(Later)

Kate Chotto kaisugimashita! Sensu to ningyō to hashi to yukata to...

Tom Daijōbu desu. Kinō nani mo kaimasen deshita. Ano kuroi fukuro no naka ni nani ga arimasu ka. Watashi no desu ka.

Kate È to... omiyage-ya ni itte, kono aoi kimono o mimashita. Kirei deshō. Ten'in wa totemo shinsetsu de Tom Cruise ni niteimashita.

Tom Tom Cruise wa dare desu ka. Kimono wa ikura deshita ka.

Kate Chotto takakatta desu ga Tōkyō de wa totemo takai desu yo!

Tom Ē! Anata wa okashikunatta n desu ka.

Kate Demo... kono gorufu no T. shatsu wa totemo yasukatta desu. Saizu gojū desu. Soshite eigo no shinbun mo kaimashita. Dōzo... ima kara terebi de sumō ga arimasu ka.

▶ New words

Learn the **New words** in half the time using flash cards. There are 22 to start you off. Get a friend to make the rest!

kaimono o shimashō *let's do some shopping*

kaimono o shimasu *do some shopping*

sā *well*

kyō *today*

shōtengai *shopping centre*

ikimashō *let's go*

...mashō *let's*

tenki *weather*

samui *cold*

terebi *TV*

sakkā *soccer, football*

tenisu *tennis*

gorufu *golf*

mōshiwake arimasen ga *I'm sorry, but...*

ikanakereba narimasen *must go*

yūbinkyoku *post office*

kitte *stamps*

katte *buy and then...*

kaimasu *buy*

kusuriya *chemist's*

dorai kurīningu *dry cleaner's*

dame *no good, not allowed*

sore *that (one)*

dake *only*

sūtsukēsu *suitcase*

kaitai desu *want to buy*

omiyage *souvenirs*

uso! *you're kidding!*

mise *shops*

mimasu *watch*

o *(marks object of sentence)*

kaisugimashita *bought too much*

sensu *folding fan*

ningyō *doll*

hashi *chopsticks*

yukata *cotton kimono*

daijōbu *no problem, it's OK*

kinō *yesterday*

nani mo *nothing*

kaimasen deshita *didn't buy*

kuroi *black*

fukuro *paper bag*

naka *in, inside*

watashi no *mine*

ē to *hmm, erm...*

aoi *blue*

deshō *don't you think?*

ten'in *shop assistant*

shinsetsu *kind*

de *and*

...ni niteimashita *looked like...*

dare *who*

deshita *was, were*

takakatta *was expensive*

yo *you know!*

anata *you*

okashikunatta *gone mad*

T. shatsu *T-shirt*

yasukatta *was cheap*

yasui *cheap*

saizu *size*

gojū *50*

eigo *English (language)*

shinbun *newspaper*

sumō *sumo wrestling*

TOTAL NEW WORDS: 65
...only 186 words to go!

Some useful extras: the colours

red	**akai/aka**	*yellow*	**kiiroi/kiiro**
blue	**aoi/ao**	*brown*	**chairo**
white	**shiroi/shiro**	*grey*	**haiiro**
black	**kuroi/kuro**	*pink*	**pinku**
green	**midori**	*orange*	**orenjiiro**

▶ Good news grammar

1 Verb forms: good news!

Remember struggling at school with all those French verb forms... *je suis*, *tu es*, *nous sommes*... And what about Italian or Spanish? No need to struggle with Japanese because the verb form does not change, regardless of who takes the action. There is one verb form for all the actions taking place now, and another one for all the actions which happened in the past. And finally there is a verb form each for saying that someone doesn't do something or *didn't* do it.

Here is a neat box with an example: *eat*

the present		the past	
eat	*don't eat*	*ate*	*didn't eat*
tabemasu	**tabemasen**	**tabemashita**	**tabemasen deshita**

Once you have learned these four verb forms you can use the pattern with all the rest. Great news!

Here's another one which you'll use every day: *be*

the present		the past	
am, are, is	*am/are/is not*	*was, were*	*was/were not*
desu	**dewa arimasen**	**deshita**	**dewa arimasen deshita**

When you use the negative form you'll often find an odd **wa** is thrown in for emphasis:

Kurejitto kādo WA tsukaemasen. *When it comes to credit cards we don't use them.*

But if you forget, it's not the end of the world. Everyone will understand you perfectly.

2 Let's do...something: *mashō*

To say: *Let's...* simply change **masu** into **mashō**. *Let's go shopping*: **kaimono o shimashō**. If you add **ka** at the end, you can turn it into a question: **Kaimono o shimashō ka**. *Shall we go shopping?*

3 *Te*: a little bad news...

Just when you thought you were home and dry with your verb forms, Kate talks about buying stamps and a little **te** pops up at the end of the verb: **kitte o katte...** *buy stamps and then...* Te is used in longer sentences when there's a verb in the middle and the sentence carries on. Here are a few examples of how verbs change when you want to say *and then...*:

ikimasu *go* – **itte** *go and then...*
tabemasu *eat* – **tabete** *eat and then...*
kaimasu *buy* – **katte** *buy and then...*

But if you want to avoid **te**, keep your sentences short!

4 *Chotto takakatta desu* – it was a bit expensive

When something happens in the past the adjective takes on the past, too.

Example   **takai** *expensive* **takakatta desu...** *was expensive*.
But don't worry if you forget.

5 *Ikanakereba narimasen*: must go

This is a bit of a mouthful but a very useful phrase. You'll learn about *must* in Week 5.

6 A reminder: always look back!

Take **fukuro no naka ni**, *inside the bag*, and then work it backwards.

▶ Learn by heart

Say these seven lines in under 50 seconds. The more expression you use the easier it will be to remember all the useful bits.

Chotto kaisugimashita!
Kyō kaimono o shimashō.
Ginkō ni ikanakereba narimasen.
Soshite omiyage o kaitai desu.
O-mise wa shichi ji made desu...
Chotto kaisugimashita!
Sensu, kimono, ningyō, o-hashi nado o kaimashita.
Demo ten`in wa totemo hansamu deshita!

▶ Let's speak Japanese

Over to you! If you have the recording, listen to check your answers. Let's start with a ten point warm up. Say in Japanese:

1 I'm sorry but I have to go.
2 Shall we do some shopping?
3 Let's go to the bank.
4 We must go to the post office.
5 I will buy a suitcase and then go to the coffee shop.
6 You're kidding! It was not Tom Cruise!
7 What! (That) was very expensive, you know!
8 I want to buy some souvenirs.
9 I want to watch sumo at 8 o'clock.
10 Sorry, we don't have a television. No problem.

Now answer in Japanese using **iie** and ...**masen deshita** (*I/we didn't...*). Change **o** to **wa**:

11 Sakkā o mimashita ka.
12 Kēki o tabemashita ka.
13 Ocha (*green tea*) o nomimashita ka.
14 Eigo no shinbun o kaimashita ka.
15 Sensu o kaimashita ka.

Finally ask some questions in Japanese. Answer them using the word in brackets.

16 How much was that T-shirt? (2,000 yen)
17 Where shall we go? (shopping centre)
18 What is inside the suitcase? (souvenirs)
19 What time is the post office (open) to? (5.30)
20 Who is Suzuki Jun? (*Japanese person* **Nihonjin**)

Answers

1 Mōshiwake arimasen ga ikanakereba narimasen.
2 Kaimono o shimashō ka.
3 Ginkō ni ikimashō.
4 Yūbinkyoku ni ikanakereba narimasen.
5 Sūtsukēsu o katte, kissaten ni ikimasu.
6 Uso! Tom Cruise dewa arimasen deshita!
7 Ē! Totemo takakatta desu yo!
8 Omiyage o kaitai desu.
9 Hachi ji ni sumō o mitai desu.
10 Sumimasen. Terebi wa arimasen. Daijōbu desu.

11 Iie, sakkā wa mimasen deshita.
12 Iie, kēki wa tabemasen deshita.
13 Iie, ocha wa nomimasen deshita.
14 Iie, eigo no shinbun wa kaimasen deshita.
15 Iie, sensu wa kaimasen deshita.
16 Ano T. shatsu wa ikura deshita ka. Nisen en deshita.
17 Doko ni ikimashō ka. Shōtengai ni ikimashō.
18 Sūtsukēsu no naka ni, nani ga arimasu ka. Omiyage ga arimasu.
19 Yūbinkyoku wa nan ji made desu ka. Go ji han made desu.
20 Suzuki Jun wa dare desu ka. Nihonjin desu.

◘ Let's speak more Japanese

For these optional exercises add an extra 15 minutes to your daily schedule. And, remember, don't worry about getting the article or endings wrong. Near enough is good enough!

In your own words

This exercise will teach you to express yourself freely. Use only the words you have learned so far.

Tell me in your own words that...

1 you would like to do the shopping today
2 you suggest going to the shopping centre
3 you must go to the bank
4 and you will buy stamps at the post office... (use **katte**)
5 ...then you want to go to the pharmacy
6 you want to buy a kimono and some chopsticks
7 you also want to buy a suitcase
8 you bought a doll, and (but) it wasn't cheap
9 you've bought a bit too much
10 you bought a kimono, dolls, fans, chopsticks...

Answers

1 Kyō kaimono o shimashō.
2 Shōtengai ni ikimashō ka.
3 Ginkō ni ikanakereba narimasen.
4 Soshite yūbinkyoku de kitte o katte...
5 ...kusuriya ni ikitai desu.
6 Kimono to hashi o kaitai desu.
7 Sūtsukēsu mo kaitai desu.
8 Ningyō o kaimashita ga chotto takakatta desu.
9 Chotto kaisugimashita.
10 Kimono to ningyō to sensu to hashi... (o kaimashita)

▶ Let's speak Japanese – fast and fluently

Translate each section and check if it is correct. Then cover the answers and say the three or four sentences fast!

20 seconds per section for a silver star, 15 seconds for a gold star.

Some of the English is in 'Japanese-speak' to help you.

Excuse me, are you buying a kimono?
This blue kimono, how much is it?
It is a bit expensive but in Tokyo it is expensive.

Sumimasen, kimono o kaimasu ka.
Kono aoi kimono wa ikura desu ka.
Chotto takai desu ga Tōkyō de wa takai desu.

Cheap suitcase I would like to buy.
What is in that black suitcase? (start with: that black suitcase)
A suitcase I have seen, but it is rather expensive.

Yasui sūtsukēsu o kaitai desu.
Ano kuroi tsūtsukēsu no naka ni nani ga arimasu ka.
Sūtsukēsu o mimashita ga chotto takai desu.

In March the weather is very bad.
Tokyo we went to. At Mitsukoshi (department store) we ate.
We had coffee and cake. It was delicious.
The waiter was very handsome and kind.

San-gatsu ni tenki ga totemo warui desu.
Tōkyō ni ikimashita. Mitsukoshi de tabemashita.
Kōhī to kēki o tabemashita. Oishikatta desu.
Uētā wa totemo hansamu de shinsetsu deshita.

Now say all the sentences in Japanese without stopping and starting. If you can do it in under one minute you are a fast and fluent winner!

But if you are not happy with your result – just try once more.

▶ Spot the keys

By now you can say many things in Japanese. But what happens if you ask a question and do not understand the answer – especially if it hits you at the speed of an automatic rifle? The smart way is not to panic and go blank but listen only for the words you know. Any familiar words which you pick up will provide you with **Key words** – clues to what the other person is saying. If you have the recording, close the book now and listen to the dialogue. Here's an example:

YOU Sumimasen, yūbinkyoku wa doko desu ka.
ANSWER *Sōdesune. Ano ... mazu* **massugu itte, ginkō** *no temae de* **migi ni magatte kudasai. Migigawa ni** *wa Yamaguchidenkiya Nishiguchichūshajōya* **o-mise** *nadoga* **arimasu. Yūbinkyoku wa** *chotto iku to-* **hidarigawa ni arimasu.** *Kōen to Fuji* **ginkō no chikaku desu yo.**

Although a lot of words were running into each other you should have managed to pick up:

massugu itte – ginkō – migi ni magatte kudasai – migigawa ni – o-mise – arimasu – yūbinkyoku wa – hidarigawa ni arimasu – ginkō no chikaku desu yo.

I think you'll get there!

Test your progress

Translate in writing. Then check the answers and be amazed!

1 Today the weather is bad. It is cold.
2 Is there a bank near here?
3 Excuse me, I must go to the post office.
4 Shall we go to a coffee shop?
5 Is football on the TV from now?
6 Where is the chemist's? Is it on the left side?
7 Hmm… It was a bit expensive but don't you think it's smart!
8 What! That was very cheap.
9 I want to watch golf and then go to work.
10 I'm sorry but we must go to the dry cleaner's.
11 The shop assistant was handsome and looked like Brad Pitt.
12 How much was it? You're kidding!
13 I want to buy an English newspaper. Let's go to the shop.
14 I ate the sandwiches but I didn't eat the cakes, you know.
15 We didn't buy anything yesterday but we bought too much today.
16 I bought dolls and cotton kimono.
17 I want to buy some stamps.
18 The room is a bit small but no problem.

19 Did you see the sumo on TV yesterday?
20 This kimono is no good. The blue kimono is beautiful.

Remember the Progress chart? You are now halfway home.

04

week four

Study for 45 minutes a day, but if you are keen try 50… 55…!

Day one

- Read **We are going to have a meal**.
- Listen to/Read **Shokuji o shimasu**.
- Listen to/Read the **New words**. Learn the easy ones.

Day two

- Repeat the dialogue. Learn the harder **New words**.
- Cut out the **Flash words** to help you.

Day three

- Learn all the **New words** until you know them well.
- Read and learn the **Good news grammar**.

Day four

- Listen to/Read **Learn by heart**.
- Cut out and learn the ten **Flash sentences**.

Day five

- Read **Say it simply**.
- Listen to/Read **Let's speak Japanese**.

Day six

- Listen to/Read **Spot the keys**.
- Listen to/Read **Let's speak more Japanese** (optional).
- Listen to/Read **Let's speak Japanese – fast and fluently** (optional).
- Translate **Test your progress**.

Day seven

Are you keeping your scores above 60%? In that case… **have a good day off!**

day-by-day guide

We are going to have a meal

Tom and Kate are now in Osaka. Mr Yamada is inviting them to dinner. (The English is in 'Japanese-speak' to get you tuned in.)

Kate Tokyo someone from, a phone call there was. A Mr Yamada or Yamaha it was. His business he didn't say.

Tom Ah, I've got it... Yamada Masaki, a company client it is. Very nice chap he is. He with appointment I have. Very important business it is.

Tom Hello, Mr Yamada is it? Tom Walker it is... yes, thank you... yes, I see... Next week, Tuesday isn't it... yes... that's right... ah, really?... yes, time I have... yes, with pleasure... when?... At nine o'clock... in front of the entrance... Right, this evening... thank you... sorry for interrupting.

Kate This evening what are we doing?

Tom Mr Yamada together with, we are going to have a meal. The restaurant is new and very good, he said. Mr Yamada my company's Edith and Peter Palmer together with, Osaka is in. (Mr Yamada is in Osaka with Edith and Peter Palmer from my company.)

Kate Edith Palmer I know. I don't like her very much. Boring and snobbish person she is. Awful dog also she owns. I suddenly ill got. Doctor call please.

Tom No way! Mr Yamada important client is. That's out of the question.

(At the restaurant)

Waiter This evening's set menu is raw fish or teriyaki steak. Bean-paste soup, rice and pickles are included.

Yamada Kate, what would you like? Fish or meat, which do you prefer?

Kate Indeed. Teriyaki steak please.

Edith Kate, for your health, meat is no good, you know.

Yamada Tom, raw fish, how about it? And drinks?

Tom Right, I raw fish set meal will go for but bean-paste soup is not wanted. And beer please.

Edith Tom, for your health, bean-paste soup is very good, you know. I love it.

⸱⸱⸱⟶ Page 52

▶ Shokuji o shimasu

Tom and Kate are now in Osaka. Mr Yamada is inviting them to dinner.

Kate Tōkyō no dare ka kara denwa ga arimashita. Yamada ka Yamaha-san deshita. Yōji o iimasen deshita.

Tom A, wakarimashita... Yamada Masaki, kaisha no o-kyakusan desu. Totemo ii kata desu. Kare to yakusoku ga arimasu. Totemo taisetsuna yōji desu.

Tom Moshi moshi, Yamada-san desu ka. Tom Walker desu... ē, arigatō gozaimasu... hai, wakarimashita... raishū no kayōbi desu ne... hai... sō desu ne... a, sō desu ka... hai, jikan arimasu... hai, zehi... itsu?... ku ji ni... iriguchi no mae... Dewa, konban... arigatō gozaimasu... shitsurei shimasu.

Kate Konban nani o shimasu ka.

Tom Yamada-san to issho ni shokuji o shimasu. Resutoran wa atarashikute totemo ii to iimashita. Yamada-san wa uchi no Edith to Peter Palmer to issho ni Ōsaka ni imasu.

Kate Edith Palmer o shitteimasu. Amari suki dewa arimasen. Taikutsu de erasōna hito desu. Hidoi inu mo katteimasu. Watashi wa kyū ni byōki ni narimashita. Isha o yonde kudasai.

Tom Dame desu yo! Yamada-san wa taisetsuna o-kyakusan desu. Sore wa dame desu.

(At the restaurant)

Waiter Konban no teishoku wa sashimi ka teriyaki sutēki de gozaimasu. Miso shiru, gohan to tsukemono mo tsuiteimasu.

Yamada Kate-san, nani ga yoroshii desu ka. O-sakana to o-niku to dochira ga ii desu ka.

Kate Sō desu ne. Teriyaki sutēki o onegaishimasu.

Edith Kate-san, kenkō no tame ni niku wa yokunai desu yo.

Yamada Tom-san, sashimi wa ikaga desu ka. Sorekara, o-nomimono wa?

Tom Ja, watashi wa sashimi teishoku ni shimasu ga miso shiru wa irimasen. Sorekara bīru o onegaishimasu.

Edith Tom-san, kenkō no tame ni miso shiru wa totemo ii desu yo. Watashi wa daisuki desu.

┅━▶ Page 53

Yamada	Edith, what would you like?
Edith	I (for me) salad and water please.
(Later)	
Yamada	Everyone, have you finished? Green tea or coffee, how about it? You're OK? Right, the bill please.
Edith	Oh, Mr Yamada, help me please. 'Doggy bag', in Japanese, what is it? I, for my dog, bag want.
Kate	Edith, your dog in England is, you know!

▶ New words

shokuji o shimasu *to have a meal*
dare ka *someone*
ka *or*
yōji *business, matter*
iimasen deshita *did not say*
iimasu *say*
a, wakarimashita *ah, I understand*
o-kyakusan *client, customer*
kata *chap, person*
kare *he*
kare to *with him*
yakusoku *appointment*
taisetsu (na) *important (arrogant)*
moshi moshi *hello (on phone)*
ē *yes*
arigatō gozaimasu *thank you*
raishū (no) *next week ('s)*
kayōbi *Tuesday*
sō desu ne *that's right*
jikan *time, hour*
zehi *I'd love to (with invitation)*
itsu *when*
iriguchi *entrance*
(no) mae *in front of*
dewa *OK, right*
konban *tonight*
shitsurei shimasu *sorry for disturbing you (said at end of call)*

issho ni *together (with)*
atarashikute *new and...*
to iimashita *he said that...*
uchi no *our (where you belong)*
o shitteimasu *I know...*
suki dewa arimasen *don't like*
taikutsu (na) *boring*
hidoi *awful*
inu *dog*
katteimasu *owns (pets)*
kyū ni *suddenly*
byōki *illness/ill*
ni narimashita *have become*
isha *doctor*
yonde kudasai *please call*
dame desu yo *no way*
teishoku *menu, set meal*
sashimi *raw fish*
sutēki *steak*
teriyaki *Japanese barbecue sauce*
miso shiru *bean-paste soup*
gohan *boiled rice*
tsukemono *Japanese pickles*
tsuiteimasu *is included*
nani ga yoroshii desu ka *what would you like? (lit. what is good?)*
o-sakana/sakana *fish*
o-niku/niku *meat*

Yamada	Edith-san, nani ga yoroshii desu ka.
Edith	Watashi wa sarada to o-mizu o onegaishimasu.
(Later)	
Yamada	Mina-san, owarimashita ka. Ocha ka kōhī wa ikaga desu ka. Yoroshii desu ka. Dewa, o-kanjō o kudasai.
Edith	Ano, Yamada-san, oshiete kudasai. 'Doggy bag' wa nihongo de nan desu ka. Watashi wa inu no tame ni baggu ga hoshii desu.
Kate	Edith-san, inu wa Igirisu ni imasu yo!

to... to *and... and*
dochira *which (of two)*
kenkō *health*
...no tame ni *for...*
yokunai *not good*
ikaga *how about/would you like?*
o-nomimono *drinks*
ni shimasu *decide on*
irimasen *don't want/need*
daisuki *love*
sarada *salad*
o-mizu/mizu *water*

mina-san *everyone*
owarimashita *finished*
ocha *green tea*
o-kanjō/kanjō *bill*
ano... *erm... (hesitation)*
oshiete kudasai *please help/tell me*
nihongo de *in Japanese*
nan desu ka *what is it?*
hoshii *want*
Igirisu *England*

TOTAL NEW WORDS: 76
...only 110 words to go!

Some easy extras

Nan yōbi desu ka *What day is it?*
Getsuyōbi *Monday*
Kayōbi *Tuesday*
Suiyōbi *Wednesday*

Mokuyōbi *Thursday*
Kinyōbi *Friday*
Doyōbi *Saturday*
Nichiyōbi *Sunday*

▶ Good news grammar

1 Like – love – want: *suki – daisuki – hoshii*

To say that you like something you use the verb **suki**. If you love something use **daisuki** (lit. 'big like'). And if you want something use **hoshii**.

Remember learning about the Japanese word order in Week 1? Remember about things being back to front? The same thing happens again, and again! This is how:

The word **wa** identifies the person who is doing the liking, loving or wanting, by following it, for example: **Watashi wa** or **Kate wa**. Then the word **ga** follows whatever Kate or I like, love or want..., for example, *dogs*: **Watashi wa/Kate wa inu ga suki desu**. If you wanted a bag you could say: **Baggu ga hoshii desu**. (You can drop the **watashi** if it's obvious that *you* want it). And if I said: **Tom wa daisuki desu**, you would know that Tom loves it. (Whatever it may be.)

If you talk about the past and say that you *liked*, *loved* or *wanted* something you would change **desu** to **deshita**, and if you didn't do any of it you would change **desu** to **dewa arimasen**. By the way, **hoshii** does something different: **hoshikatta desu** means *I wanted* and **hoshikunai desu** means *I don't want* (you have already met this in Weeks 2 and 3).

2 – *Kute* and *de*

Resutoran wa atarashikute totemo ii: *The restaurant is new and very nice*. To say *and* when joining two adjectives – **atarashii** and **ii** – you use **kute**. Take off the last letter of the first word, add – **kute** and there you have it: **atarashikute totemo ii**, *new and very nice*.

Sometimes **de** is used to say *and*. But don't worry about which to use when. If you pick the wrong one it's not that serious.

3 *Ii* – good, nice, OK

This is an odd one but worth learning:

good: **ii**   *is not good*: **yokunai**   *was good*: **yokatta**
good and...: **yokute**

4 *To iimasu – to iimashita*

This means: *I, you, we* etc. *say* or *said that...*

Example   **Totemo ii to iimashita**: *He said that it is very nice*.
Remember to go backwards!

▶ Learn by heart (1)

Pretend this is a telephone call by a rather opinionated person. When you have learned it by heart try to act it out in under 90 seconds.

> ### *Watashi wa totemo omoshiroi hito desu.*
> ### I am a very interesting person.
>
> Konban issho ni shokuji o shimashō.
> Totemo ii resutoran o shitteimasu. Wain wa totemo oishii desu.
> Dame desu ka.
> Dōshite[1]? Watashi wa totemo omoshiroi hito desu yo.
> Watashi o shitteimasu ka.
> Sō desu. Terebi no sutā[2] desu.
> Tenki yohō[3]- watashi desu!
> Dekimasen ka. Dōshite desu ka.
> Yōji ga arimasu ka.
> Are! Ii chansu[4] desu yo!

[1]*why* [2]*star* [3]*weather forecast* [4]*chance, opportunity*

If you are short of time this week, you can settle for the shorter piece which follows... or you could do both!

▶ Learn by heart (2)

> ### *Amari suki dewa arimasen.* I don't like him very much.
> Yamamoto Hiroshi-san o shitteimasu ka.
> Issho ni resutoran ni ikanakereba narimasen.
> Dōshite? Totemo taisetsuna o-kyakusan desu kara.
> Demo amari suki dewa arimasen.
> Itsu?
> Konban! Terebi de sakkā ga arimasu!
> Iya desu!*

*when you don't want to do something

▶ Spot the keys

You practised listening for key words when you asked the way to the post office in Week 3. Now you are in a department store and you ask the sales assistant if the blue T-shirt you fancy is available in size 38.

This is what you could say:

> **Sumimasen, kono aoi T. shatsu wa saizu sanjū hachi mo arimasu ka.**

She asks you to wait a moment **Chotto matte kudasai** then goes away. This is what she says when she comes back:

> *O-matase shimashita. Honsha ni* **denwa** *itashimashita ga* **saizu san jū hachi** *no wa* **kuroi** *no dake gozaimasu. O-kyakusama nara* **san jū roku demo daijōbu** *da to omoimasu.* **Sanjū roku** *nara* **aoi** *no ga gozaimasu.*

Size 38 was only available in black but she thinks size 36 will be all right and they have this in blue.

▶ Let's speak Japanese

Here are ten sentences as a warm-up.

1 I do not like the client.
2 Do we go with him?
3 Which do you prefer, fish or meat?
4 Yes, with pleasure (I'd love to).
5 Do you have an appointment?
6 I like dogs.
7 I know a cheap restaurant.
8 My company is five minutes from here.
9 Fish is very good for you (for your health).
10 Can you help me/tell me, please?

Now pretend you are in Japan with friends who don't speak Japanese. They say: *Please ask…*

11 if he knows a good restaurant.
12 if he likes raw fish.
13 what he wants to drink.
14 whether he would like beer.
15 whether he prefers beer or water.

On another occasion they will say: *Please tell her…*

16 that the bean-paste soup is not very hot.
17 that you don't like meat.
18 that you know her phone number.
19 that you don't want (need) rice.
20 to call a doctor.

Answers

1 O-kyakusan wa suki dewa arimasen.
2 Kare to issho ni ikimasu ka.
3 O-sakana to o-niku to dochira ga ii desu ka.
4 Hai, zehi.
5 Yakusoku ga arimasu ka.
6 Inu ga suki desu.
7 Yasui resutoran o shitteimasu.
8 (Uchi no) kaisha wa koko kara go-fun desu.
9 Kenkō no tame ni sakana ga totemo ii desu.
10 Oshiete kudasai.
11 Ii resutoran o shitteimasu ka.
12 Sashimi ga suki desu ka.
13 O-nomimono wa (nani ga yoroshii desu ka).
14 Bīru wa ikaga desu ka.
15 Bīru to o-mizu to dochira ga ii desu ka.
16 Miso shiru wa amari atsukunai desu.
17 Niku wa suki dewa arimasen.
18 O-denwa-bangō o shitteimasu.
19 Gohan wa irimasen.
20 Isha o yonde kudasai.

▶ Let's speak more Japanese

In your own words

This exercise will teach you to express yourself freely. Use only the words you have learned so far.

Tell me in your own words that...

1 somebody knows the number of Mr Yamada
2 you have important business with him
3 you would like to know if I know him
4 he is a very good and arrogant client
5 you have an appointment with him next week
6 you are going out to eat with Mr Yamada on Saturday
7 Edith Palmer has become ill; get someone to call a doctor
8 you are very fond of rice and Japanese pickles
9 you eat fish for your health
10 you were in the restaurant until eleven o'clock (*were in* **imashita**)

Answers

1 Dare ka ga Yamada-san no denwa-bangō o shitteimasu.
2 Kare to taisetsuna yōji ga arimasu.
3 Kare o shitteimasu ka.
4 Totemo yokute erasōna o-kyakusan desu.
5 Raishū kare to yakusoku ga arimasu.
6 Doyōbi ni Yamada-san to issho ni shokuji o shimasu.
7 Edith Palmer-san wa byōki ni narimashita. Isha o yonde kudasai.
8 Gohan to tsukemono ga daisuki desu.
9 Kenkō no tame ni sakana o tabemasu.
10 Jūichi-ji made resutoran ni imashita.

▶ Let's speak Japanese – fast and fluently

Translate each section and check if it is correct. Then cover the answers and say the three or four sentences fast!

20 seconds per section for a silver star, 15 seconds for a gold star.

Some of the English is in 'Japanese-speak' to help you.

Mr Yamada you know? Today phone call there was.
His business he didn't say.
It was for an appointment on Wednesday.

Yamada-san o shitteimasu ka. Kyō denwa ga arimashita.
Yōji o iimasen deshita.
Raishū no suiyōbi ni yakusoku ga arimasu.

A new restaurant there is. In front of the bank it is.
It is pokey (narrow) and expensive, he said.
But (**demo**) tonight, at my house, with him, I would like to eat.

Atarashii resutoran ga arimasu. Ginkō no mae desu (or **ni arimasu**).
Semakute takai to iimashita.
Demo konban, watashi no ie de, kare to, tabetai desu.

Unfortunately, you must go.
My dog suddenly got ill. For his health meat is not good.
Oh, really? 'Poor thing' in Japanese what is it? ('Kawaiso.')

Mōshiwake arimasen ga ikanakereba narimasen.
Inu ga kyū ni byōki ni narimashita. Kenkō no tame ni niku wa yokunai desu (or **dame desu**).
Ā sō desu ka. 'Poor thing' nihongo de nan desu ka. 'Kawaiso'.

Now say all the sentences in Japanese without stopping and starting. If you can do it in under one minute you are a fast and fluent winner!

But if you are not happy with your result – just try once more.

Say it simply

When people want to speak Japanese but don't dare it's usually because they are trying to *translate* what they want to say from English into Japanese. But because they don't know some of the words they give up!

With **Instant Japanese** you work around the words you don't know with the words you know. And some 400 words is enough to say anything! It may not always be very elegant – but who cares? You are *communicating*!

Here are two examples showing you how to say things simply. I have **highlighted** the words which are not part of the **Instant** vocabulary.

1 In English:
You need to **change** your **flight** to London from Tuesday to Friday. **Say it simply:**

Sumimasen, kayōbi ni yōji (or yakusoku) ga arimasu kara kinyōbi ni London ni ikitai n desu. (*Excuse me, I have an appointment on Tuesday and so I want to go to London on Friday.*)

Or: **Sumimasen, kayōbi wa dame desu. Kinyōbi ni London ni ikitai desu.** (*Excuse me, Tuesday is no good. I want to go to London on Friday.*)

2 You are **lost** in Tokyo and **need to find** a phone and **let** your friend **know** where you are. **Say it simply:**

Sumimasen, koko wa doko desu ka. Kono chikaku ni (kōshū) denwa ga arimasu ka. (*Excuse me, this place where is it? Near here is there a (public) phone?*)

Or: **Sumimasen, koko wa doko desu ka. (Kōshū) denwa wa doko desu ka.** (*Excuse me, this place where is it? Public phone where is it?*)

Test your progress

Translate into Japanese:

1 He said that the shop is expensive and not very good.
2 He didn't say his phone number.
3 She said that the restaurant is a little narrow (small).
4 I know a cheap and nice souvenir shop.
5 How about green tea? And would you like rice?
6 Which would you prefer, black tea or coffee?
7 What is it? You don't want pickles?
8 I love fish. I will go for the raw fish.
9 I don't like red meat. Salad and beer please.
10 I saw Sawada Akiko on the TV. She is a very interesting person.
11 There was a phone call from the company. It is an important matter.
12 Sorry, I have an appointment and so I don't have time. (*and so* **kara**)
13 I had a meal with him yesterday. He is a very nice chap.
14 Call the doctor, I've become ill.
15 Please help me. What is *ice cream* in Japanese?
16 I drink water for my health.
17 What are we doing next week? I want to go to the shopping centre.
18 I don't like this bean-paste soup. It is awful!
19 Next Tuesday I am going to a new restaurant with Miss Morita.
20 We worked until late. We finished at 11.30.

How are your 'shares' looking on the Progress chart? Going up?

05

week five

How about 20 minutes on the train, tube or bus, 15 minutes on the way home and 20 minutes before switching on the television...?

Day one

- Read **Travelling**.
- Listen to/Read **Ryokō**.
- Listen to/Read the **New words**. Learn 15 or more.

Day two

- Repeat the dialogue. Learn the harder **New words**.
- Cut out the **Flash words** to get stuck in.

Day three

- Test yourself to perfection on all the **New words**.
- Read and learn the **Good news grammar**.

Day four

- Listen to/Read **Learn by heart**.
- Cut out and learn the ten **Flash sentences**.

Day five

- Listen to/Read **Let's speak Japanese**.
- Go over **Learn by heart**.

Day six

- Listen to/Read **Spot the keys**.
- Listen to/Read **Let's speak more Japanese** (optional).
- Listen to/Read **Let's speak Japanese – fast and fluently** (optional).
- Translate **Test your progress**.

Day seven

I bet you don't want a day off... but I insist!

day-by-day guide

Travelling

Tom and Kate are now travelling through Japan by train, bus and hired car. They talk to the ticket clerk (**Eki-in**), at the station, to Jim on the train and later to the bus driver (**Untenshu**). (The English is in 'Japanese-speak' to get you tuned in.)

(At the station)

Tom	Hiroshima-bound tickets, two items, please.
Eki-in	Is that one way? Or is that return?
Tom	Excuse me, more slowly speak please.
Eki-in	One-way-or-return?
Tom	One way please. The next train what time is it? What number platform is it?
Eki-in	9.45, number six platform.
Kate	Tom, this no-smoking carriage in, vacant seats there are. Hey! That person cigarette is smoking. Excuse me, this (place) no-smoking carriage is. Cigarettes are not allowed.
Jim	Sorry, I don't understand. I'm from England.

(At the bus stop)

Kate	The Miyajima-bound bus 20 minutes past 1 at, comes. Tom, these postcards and letters, that post box in, put please. I photographs will take. It's nice weather and so it's beautiful.
Tom	Kate, quickly, buses, two vehicles, are coming. This one full is. That one full isn't. Miyajima to two items please.
Utenshu	This bus Hiroshima to is.
Tom	What! This is Hiroshima.
Utenshu	But this bus Hiroshima hospital to is.

(In the car)

Tom	That one our rental car is. Three days 10,000 yen is. Cheap and good isn't it.
Kate	That car I don't like. It is very old and so it is very cheap. If there are no problems it'll be lucky.
Tom	But the first car was too expensive, the second one was too big. This one is just right you know.

(Later)

Map there isn't. This place where is it?

······➡ Page 66

▶ Ryokō

Tom and Kate are now travelling through Japan by train, bus and hired car. They talk to the ticket clerk (**Eki-in**), at the station, to Jim on the train and later to the bus driver (**Untenshu**).

(At the station)

Tom   Hiroshima-yuki no kippu o nimai kudasai.

Eki-in   Katamichi desu ka. Ōfuku desu ka.

Tom   Sumimasen, motto yukkuri itte kudasai.

Eki-in   Ka-ta-mi-chi ka o-o-fu-ku desu ka.

Tom   Katamichi o onegaishimasu. Tsugi no densha wa nan ji desu ka. Nan ban sen desu ka.

Eki-in   Ku ji yonjūgo-hun sugi, roku ban sen desu.

Kate   Tom, kono kin'ensha ni kūseki ga arimasu. Are! Ano hito wa tabako o sutteimasu. Sumimasen, koko wa kin'ensha desu. Tabako wa dame desu.

Jim   Sorry, I don't understand. I'm from Igirisu.

(At the bus stop)

Kate   Miyajima-yuki no basu wa ichi ji nijuppun ni kimasu. Tom, kono ehagaki to tegami o ano posuto ni dashite kudasai. Watashi wa shashin o torimasu. Ii tenki desu kara kirei desu.

Tom   Kate, hayaku, basu ga ni dai kimasu. Kore wa man'in desu. Are wa man'in dewa arimasen. Miyajima made nimai kudasai.

Untenshu   Kono basu wa Hiroshima made desu.

Tom   Are! Koko wa Hiroshima desu.

Untenshu   Demo kono basu wa Hiroshima byōin made desu.

(In the car)

Tom   Are ga watashitachi no renta kā desu. Mikkakan de ichi man en desu. Yasukute ii desu ne.

Kate   Ano kuruma wa suki dewa arimasen. Totemo furui kara totemo yasui desu yo. Mondai ga nai to ii desu ne.

Tom   Demo ichiban-me no kuruma wa takasugite, niban-me no wa ōkisugimashita. Kore wa chōdo ii desu yo.

(Later)

Chizu ga arimasen. Koko wa doko desu ka.

┉┉➤ Page 67

The motorway where is it? On the left side petrol station and bus stop there is. On the right side school there is. Quickly!

Kate   Over there go please. Traffic lights beyond. Then right turn please.

(On the motorway)

Why this car speed doesn't get up? Petrol is there enough? How many litres are there? Oil is enough? Engine isn't too hot? This car is no good, you know. Mobile phone, where is it? Rental car company's phone number, what number is it? My handbag where is it?

Tom   Kate, my head hurts, you know. What! The rain is falling. Why the police at the rear are?

▶ New words

yuki *bound for*
kippu *tickets*
nimai *two items*
katamichi *one way*
ōfuku *return*
yukkuri *slowly*
itte kudasai *please say*
tsugi (no) *the next*
densha *train*
nan ban sen (*lit. what number line/platform?*)
kin'ensha *no smoking carriage*
kūseki *vacant (seats)*
are! *hey!, what!*
hito *person*
tabako *cigarettes*
sutteimasu *is smoking*
basu *bus*
Miyajima (*island off Hiroshima, has bridges*)
nijuppun *20 (minutes) past*
ehagaki *picture postcard*
e *picture*
tegami *letter*
posuto *post box*
dashite kudasai *please post*

shashin *photographs*
torimasu *take*
hayaku *quickly*
ni dai *two vehicles*
kimasu *is/are coming*
kore *this one*
are *that one (over there)*
man'in *full*
byōin *hospital*
renta kā *rental car*
mikkakan *for three days*
man *10,000*
ichi man en *10,000 yen*
kuruma *car*
furui *old*
mondai ga nai to *if there isn't a problem*
ii desu ne *we'll be lucky*
ichiban-me *the first*
niban-me *the second*
takasugite *too expensive (and)*
ōkisugimashita *too big*
ōkii *big*
chōdo ii *just right*
chizu *map*
kōsoku dōro *motorway*

Kōsoku dōro wa doko desu ka. Hidarigawa ni gasorin sutando to basu tei ga arimasu. Migigawa ni gakkō ga arimasu. Hayaku!

Kate   Asoko ni itte kudasai. Shingō no saki desu. Sorekara migi ni magatte kudasai.

(On the motorway)

Dōshite kono kuruma wa supīdo ga demasen ka. Gasorin ga tarimasu ka. Nan rittoru arimasu ka. Oiru ga tarimasu ka. Enjin wa atsusugimasen ka. Kono kuruma wa dame desu yo. Keitai denwa wa doko desu ka. Renta kā no kaisha no denwa bangō wa nanban desu ka. Watashi no handobaggu wa doko desu ka.

Tom   Kate, atama ga itai desu yo. Are! Ame ga futteimasu. Dōshite keisatsu ga ushiro ni imasu ka.

gasorin sutando *petrol station*	**oiru** *oil*
basu tei *bus stop*	**atsusugimasu** *too hot*
gakkō *school*	**atsui** *hot*
asoko *over there*	**handobaggu** *handbag*
shingō *traffic lights*	**atama** *head*
saki *beyond*	**itai** *hurts*
demasu *get up (speed)*	**ame** *rain*
supīdo *speed*	**futteimasu** *is falling*
tarimasu ka *is there enough?*	**dōshite** *why*
tarimasu *enough*	**keisatsu** *police*
rittoru *litres*	**ushiro** *at the rear*

TOTAL NEW WORDS: 71
…only 39 words to go!

▶ Good news grammar

1 *Te* and *kudasai*: please do something!

Remember the **te** in Week 3 which was used in long sentences? Here's another **te**, joined by **kudasai** *please*. Te + kudasai means: *Please do something!*

Itte kudasai, oshiete kudasai, dashite kudasai. *Please go/tell/put.*

2 My, ours, his, hers: *no*

This is really easy. Just add **no** after **watashi** for *my* and after **watashitachi** for *our*: **Watashi no, watashitachi no.** If it is *Kate's* say: **Kate-san no.**

3 Shortcut

If you want to say *one* like in the *second one* or *my one* or *mine* (or *his, hers* or *ours*) you can simply say **wa**. This will save you repeating *car, travel agent* or whatever you may be talking about. So, **niban-me no kuruma** becomes **niban-me no wa**: *the second one*.

4 *Sugimasu – sugimashita*: too... (very useful)

Think how often you say: *too big, too hot* or *too much*. In Japanese you simply use **sugimasu** for *–is too...*, and **sugimashita** for *–was too...* With adjectives, attach it to the end: **kirei – kireisugimasu**: *is too beautiful*. With some of them, like **ōkii** *big* or **takai** *expensive* you'll have to drop the **i** first ...**takasugimasu**. With verbs, put it in the place of **masu**: **tabemasu – tabesugimashita**: *ate too much*.

5 *This* and *that*, and *that over there*

Here are nine little words worth remembering:

kore *this* (one)	**sore** *that* (one)	**are** *that* (one) over there
kono basu *this bus*	**sono basu** *that bus*	**ano basu** *that bus* over there
koko *this place*	**soko** *that place*	**asoko** *that place* over there

The first line shows you the words for *this, that* and *that over there* when they are **used on their own**. In the second line they are used **with a noun**, like bus: *this bus, that bus* etc.

And in the third line you'll find three special words used only with **place**. Quite easy really, once you know them!

6 Preview: I must work

In Week 6 there won't be any new grammar, just a neat table to remind you of your verbs. But there's a small point in the dialogue that's worth noting: Remember learning *must go* in Week 2? Have a quick look back. Here's another tongue twister, or – how to say *must make* or *must do*, like *do work*, *do golf* or *make (a) phonecall*: You say **shinakereba narimasen**. So, if you must play golf instead of doing work say: **gorufu o shinakereba narimasen**.

▶ Learn by heart

Someone has crashed the car and someone else is getting suspicious...! Try to say these lines fluently and like a prize-winning play!

Tenisu o mimashō ka

A Tenisu o mimashō ka.
Tōkyō kyōgi jō[1] de tenisu no gēmu[2] ga arimasu.
Amerika-jin no senshu[3] o mitai desu.
Basu ka densha de[4] ikimashō ka.
B Basu ka densha desu ka. Dōshite?
Asoko ni ii kuruma ga arimasu yo.
A Ē to... ame ga futteimashita. Soshite aka shingō o mimasen deshita. Daijōbu deshita ga... Amari hidokunai.
Seibishi[5] wa totemo shinsetsu deshita!

---

[1]*sports ground;* [2]*game;* [3]*player;* [4]*by bus or train;* [5]*mechanic*

▶ Let's speak Japanese

Here's your ten point warm-up. Respond to the answers with a question, referring to the words in CAPITAL LETTERS.

1 Keitai denwa wa HANDOBAGGU NO NAKA ni arimasu.
2 Asoko ni KŌSOKU DŌRO ga arimasu.
3 ICHI JI NIJUPPUN ni basu ga kimasu.
4 KEISATSU ga shingō no saki ni arimasu.
5 Hiroshima made ICHI MAN EN desu.
6 TOTEMO FURUI KARA kono apāto wa suki dewa arimasen.
7 KURUMA de Igirisu ni ikimasu.
8 AKA SHINGŌ o mimasen deshita.
9 IIE, densha wa suki dewa arimasen.
10 HAI, gakkō ga suki desu.

Now answer starting with **hai** then try again using **iie:**

11 Densha no kippu ga arimasu ka.
12 Basu ga kimasu ka.
13 Koko wa kin'ensha desu ka.
14 Kōhī o nomisugimashita ka.
15 Enjin ga atsusugimasu ka.

Reply to these questions with **hai** and using *this* and *that* correctly:

16 Kore wa Suzuki-san no kuruma desu ka.
17 Sono basu wa Kyōto-yuki desu ka.
18 Ano hito wa uchi no kaisha de hataraiteimasu ka.
19 Sumimasen, soko wa kūseki desu ka.
20 Soko wa samusugimasu ka.

Answers

1 Keitai denwa wa doko ni arimasu ka (doko desu ka).
2 Asoko ni nani ga arimasu ka.
3 Nan ji ni basu ga kimasu ka.
4 Nani ga shingō no saki ni arimasu ka.
5 Hiroshima made ikura desu ka.
6 Dōshite kono apāto wa suki dewa arimasen ka.
7 Nan/nani de Igirisu ni ikimasu ka.
8 Nani o mimasen deshita ka.
9 Densha ga suki desu ka.
10 Gakkō ga suki desu ka.
11 Hai, densha no kippu ga arimasu (iie, arimasen).
12 Hai, basu ga kimasu (iie, kimasen).
13 Hai, koko wa kin'ensha desu (iie, kin'ensha dewa arimasen).
14 Hai, kōhī o nomisugimashita (iie, nomisugimasen deshita).
15 Hai, enjin ga atsusugimasu (iie, atsusugimasen).
16 Hai, sore wa Suzuki-san no kuruma desu.
17 Hai, kono basu wa Kyōto-yuki desu.
18 Hai, ano hito wa uchi no kaisha de hataraiteimasu.
19 Hai, koko wa kūseki desu.
20 Hai, koko wa samusugimasu.

▶ Let's speak more Japanese

In your own words

This exercise will teach you to express yourself freely. Use only the words you have learned so far.

Tell me in your own words that...

1 you bought a return ticket to Hiroshima
2 the next train is at 10.15
3 there are empty seats in non smoking
4 on Monday you will go by bus to the hospital
5 you must make a phone call to your company
6 this bus is full; that one isn't
7 over there is your rental car; it is new and very cheap
8 your wife says 'This car is terrible, I don't like it'
9 she says the car is too slow (can't get up speed) and the engine overheats
10 if there isn't a problem you'll be lucky

Answers

1 Hiroshima-yuki no ōfuku kippu o kaimashita.
2 Tsugi no densha wa jū-ji han desu.
3 Kin'ensha ni kūseki ga arimasu.
4 Getsuyōbi ni basu de byōin ni ikimasu.
5 Kaisha ni denwa o shinakereba narimasen.
6 Kono basu wa man'in desu. Sore wa man'in dewa arimasen.
7 Are ga (or **Are wa**) watashi no renta kā desu. Atarashikute totemo yasui desu.
8 Tsuma wa: 'Kono kuruma wa hidoi desu. Suki dewa arimasen' to iimasu.
9 '(Kono kuruma wa) supīdo ga demasen. Enjin wa atsusugimasu' to iimasu.
10 Mondai ga nai to ii desu ne.

▶ Let's speak Japanese – fast and fluently

Translate each section and check if it is correct. Then cover the answers and say the three or four sentences fast!

25 seconds per section for a silver star, 20 seconds for a gold star.

Some of the English is in 'Japanese-speak' to help you.

An Ōsaka-bound ticket, one please. One way please.
How much? I am sorry, more slowly speak please.
Yes, a smoking carriage seat please. (use **seki** or **kippu**)

Ōsaka-yuki no kippu o ichimai kudasai. Katamichi o onegaishimasu.
Ikura desu ka. Sumimasen, motto yukkuri itte kudasai.
Hai, kin'ensha no seki / kippu o kudasai (o onegaishimasu).

My wife, that post box, photo is going to take.
In England the post boxes are red.
Unfortunately, this bus is full.
These postcards, that postbox in, please put.

Tsuma wa ano posuto no shashin o torimasu.
Igirisu de wa posuto ga akai desu.
Mōshiwake arimasen ga kono basu wa man'in desu.
Kono hagaki wa sono posuto ni dashite kudasai.

Tokyo map we don't have.
The motorway where is it?
On the left a bus there is. On the right the police there is.
My wife has a headache.
Where is this?

Tōkyō no chizu ga arimasen.
Kōsoku dōro wa doko desu ka.
Hidarigawa ni basu ga arimasu. Migigawa ni keisatsu ga imasu.
Tsuma wa atama ga itai desu.
Koko wa doko desu ka.

Now say all the sentences in Japanese without stopping and starting. If you can do it in under one minute you are a fast and fluent winner!

But if you are not happy with your result – just try once more.

◨ Spot the keys

This time you plan a trip in the country. What about the weather? This is what you could ask:

Sumimasen, kyō no tenki wa dō desu ka.

Here's the answer:

Dō-ka nā. Hakkiri **wakarimasen ga terebi no tenki yōhō** *ni yoru to ichinichi jū* **atsukute, sanjū** *do da sō desu.* **Konban chotto ame** *ga furu sō desu.*

She doesn't know for sure but according to the TV weather forecast it will be hot – 30 degrees – with a little rain this evening.

Test your progress

Translate into Japanese:

1 May I have three tickets for Tokyo (Tokyo-bound) please?
2 I don't like this bus. It is too old.
3 How much does the return (ticket) cost?
4 What is it? Speak more slowly please.
5 This is a school. Cigarettes (ie: smoking) are not allowed, you know.
6 Quickly, the train is coming. It's platform three.
7 Put the postcards in this post box. Is the post box red? That's right.
8 Cars or trains, which do you like better?
9 There wasn't enough petrol but I didn't see the petrol station.
10 There is a chemist's over there. It's near the bus stop.
11 I would like two single tickets. The non-smoking car please.
12 She is always smoking. It's not good for her health.
13 The motorway is awful! I am going to take the train.
14 Where is my mobile phone? Call the police!
15 It is raining at the moment in England but it is too hot in Japan!
16 He will come to Japan next week.
17 I like Mr Suzuki's Toyota Celica. Was it expensive?
18 The first bus was full but the second one was not full.
19 Go over there. Beyond the bus stop. On the left side is a school.
20 I have a headache and so I haven't eaten anything!

If you know all your words you should score over 80%!

06

week six

This is your last week! Need I say more?

Day one

- Read **At the airport**.
- Listen to/Read **Kūkō de**.
- Listen to/Read the **New words**. There are only a handful!

Day two

- Repeat **Kūkō de**. Learn all the **New words**.
- Work with the **Flash words** and **Flash sentences**.

Day three

- Test yourself on the **Flash sentences**.
- Listen to/Read and learn **Sayōnara!**

Day four

- No more **Good news grammar!** Have a look at the summary.
- Read **Say it simply**.

Day five

- Listen to/Read **Spot the keys**.
- Listen to/Read **Let's speak Japanese**.

Day six

- Listen to/Read **Let's speak more Japanese** (optional).
- Listen to/Read **Let's speak Japanese – fast and fluently** (optional).
- Your last **Test your progress**! Go for it!

Day seven

Congratulations!

You have successfully completed the course and can now speak

Instant Japanese!

At the airport

Tom and Kate are on their way back to Birmingham. At Tokyo airport they meet an old friend… (The English is in 'Japanese-speak' to get you tuned in.)

Tom　　Monday from work must do. Awful it is. From here Hong Kong or Hawaii to I want to go. I where am, the company doesn't know, so shall we go?

Kate　　My colleagues what will they do you think? Perhaps three days they will wait and then my mother to phone. My mother the mobile phone number will teach/tell. And then?

Tom　　Yes, yes I understand. At Christmas let's travel. By boat Madeira to, let's go… Right, newspaper I buy… Kate, look! Suzuki Jun it is.

Jun　　Hello. How are you? Why this place to have you come? This my wife Nancy is. Your holiday is already over? How was it?

Kate　　Japan a wonderful country is. A lot of sightseeing we did but we ate too much. Now Osaka and Hiroshima and Kyoto about well we understand/know.

Jun　　Next year Hokkaido to go please. Kate, my wife computer book wants to buy. Could you help her please? Tom, together beer would you like to drink?

(In the bookshop)

Kate　　A good book there isn't, is there. Your husband with England to are you going?

Nancy　　No, Osaka to (as far as) we are going. Jun's mother there lives. Tomorrow train by we return. More cheap because (reason why).

Kate　　Your husband Honda at works doesn't he.

Nancy　　That's right. The work interesting is but the salary not very good is. Our car old is. The apartment also old and small is. My parents and my friend also America in live and so often letters I write. America to visit I want to go but it's too expensive.

Kate　　But Hokkaido in apartment you have, don't you.

Nancy　　A Hokkaido apartment? I Hokkaido to have never been. Hokkaido is too expensive because.

Tom　　Kate, come on! Shortly we depart. Goodbye… Kate, what's the matter? Suzuki's wife something said?

Kate　　Wait! Tom, wait!

Tom and Kate are on their way back to Birmingham. At Tokyo airport they meet an old friend…

Tom	Getsuyōbi kara shigoto o shinakereba narimasen. Hidoi desu. Korekara Hong Kong ka Hawaii ni ikitai desu. Watashi ga doko ni iru ka kaisha wa shirimasen kara ikimashō ka.
Kate	Watashi no dōryō wa dō suru to omoimasu ka. Tabun mikkakan matte, sorekara haha ni denwa shimasu. Haha wa keitai denwa no denwa bangō o oshiemasu. Sorekara?
Tom	Hai, hai, wakarimashita. Kurisumasu ni ryokō shimashō. Fune de Madeira ni ikimashō… ja, shinbun o kaimasu… Kate, mite! Suzuki Jun-san desu.
Jun	Konnichiwa. O-genki desu ka. Dōshite koko ni kimashita ka. Kore wa tsuma no Nancy desu. O-yasumi wa mō owarimashita ka. Dō deshita ka.
Kate	Nihon wa subarashii kuni desu. Takusan kankō shimashita ga tabesugimashita. Ima Ōsaka to Hiroshima to Kyōto no koto ga yoku wakarimasu.
Jun	Rainen Hokkaidō ni itte kudasai. Kate-san, tsuma wa konpyūta no hon o kaitai desu. Tetsudatte kudasaimasen ka. Tom-san, issho ni bīru o nomimasen ka.

(In the bookshop)

Kate	Ii hon ga arimasen ne. Go-shujin to Igirisu ni ikimasu ka.
Nancy	Iie, Ōsaka made ikimasu. Jun no okāsan ga soko ni sundeimasu. Ashita densha de modorimasu. Motto yasui kara.
Kate	Go-shujin wa Honda de hataraiteimasu ne.
Nancy	Sō desu. Shigoto wa omoshiroi desu ga kyūryō wa amari yokunai desu. Uchi no kuruma wa furui desu. Apāto mo furukute semai desu. Watashi no ryōshin mo tomodachi mo Amerika ni sundeimasu kara yoku tegami o kakimasu. Amerika ni ikitai desu ga takasugimasu.
Kate	Demo Hokkaidō ni apāto ga arimasu ne.
Nancy	Hokkaidō no apāto desu ka. Watashi wa Hokkaidō ni itta koto ga arimasen. Hokkaidō wa takasugimasu kara.
Tom	Kate, kite! Sorosoro shuppatsu shimasu. Sayōnara… Kate, dōshita n desu ka. Suzuki-san no okusan wa nani ka iimashita ka.
Kate	Matte! Tom, matte!

▶ New words

kūkō *airport*
shinakereba narimasen *must do*
korekara *after this*
doko ni iru ka *where I am*
shirimasen *don't know*
dōryō *colleagues*
dō suru *what will they do*
omoimasu *think*
tabun *perhaps*
haha *my mother*
denwa shimasu *phone*
oshiemasu *tell, teach*
kurisumasu *Christmas*
fune de *by boat*
mite *look*
o-genki *are you well?*
mō *already*
subarashii *wonderful*
kuni *country*
takusan *a lot*
kankō *sightseeing*
-no koto *about...*

yoku wakarimasu *I know/understand very well*
rainen *next year*
hon *book*
tetsudatte kudasaimasen ka *could you kindly give her a hand*
go-shujin *someone else's husband*
okāsan *someone else's mother*
modorimasu *return*
kyūryō *salary*
kakimasu *write*
itta koto ga arimasen *I have never been*
kite! *come on!*
sorosoro *shortly*
shuppatsu shimasu *depart*
sayōnara *goodbye*
dōshita n desu ka *what's up?*
okusan *someone else's wife*
nani ka *something*

TOTAL NEW WORDS: 39
TOTAL JAPANESE WORDS LEARNED: 388
EXTRA WORDS: 57

GRAND TOTAL: 445

Good news grammar

As promised there is no new grammar in this lesson, just a summary of the most useful **Instant** *verbs* which appear in the six weeks. This is not for learning, just for a quick check. You know and have used most of them!

Verb	Present/Future	Past	Negative	Negative Past
	masu	mashita	masen	masen deshita
wait	machimasu	machimashita	machimasen	machimasen deshita
go	ikimasu	ikimashita	ikimasen	ikimasen deshita
come	kimasu	kimashita	kimasen	kimasen deshita
phone	denwa shimasu	denwa shimashita	denwa shimasen	denwa shimasen deshita
do	shimasu	shimashita	shimasen	shimasen deshita
eat	tabemasu	tabemashita	tabemasen	tabemasen deshita
drink	nomimasu	nomimashita	nomimasen	nomimasen deshita
do shopping	kaimono o shimasu	kaimono o shimashita	kaimono o shimasen	kaimono o shimasen deshita
buy	kaimasu	kaimashita	kaimasen	kaimasen deshita
have a meal	shokuji o shimasu	shokuji o shimashita	shokuji o shimasen	shokuji o shimasen deshita
say	iimasu	iimashita	iimasen	iimasen deshita
write	kakimasu	kakimashita	kakimasen	kakimasen deshita
understand	wakarimasu	wakarimashita	wakarimasen	wakarimasen deshita
become	narimasu	narimashita	narimasen	narimasen deshita
call	yomimasu	yomimashita	yomimasen	yomimasen deshita
finish	owarimasu	owarimashita	owarimasen	owarimasen deshita
need	irimasu	irimashita	irimasen	irimasen deshita
take	torimasu	torimashita	torimasen	torimasen deshita
put, post	dashimasu	dashimashita	dashimasen	dashimasen deshita
be enough	tarimasu	tarimashita	tarimasen	tarimasen deshita
teach/tell	oshiemasu	oshiemashita	oshiemasen	oshiemasen deshita
return	modorimasu	modorimashita	modorimasen	modorimasen deshita
depart	shuppatsu shimasu	shuppatsu shimashita	shuppatsu shimasen	shuppatsu shimasen deshita
travel	ryokō shimasu	ryokō shimashita	ryokō shimasen	ryokō shimasen deshita
sightseeing	kankō shimasu	kankō shimashita	kankō shimasen	kankō shimasen deshita

▶ Learn by heart

This is your last dialogue to **Learn by heart**. Give it your best!

You now have six prize-winning party pieces, and a large store of everyday sayings which will be very useful.

Sayōnara...!

Kate	Moshi moshi, Yamada-san? Kate Walker desu.
	Ima Narita kūkō ni imasu.
	Yasumi wa mō owarimashita.
	Kono aida wa* arigatō gozaimashita.
	Tom wa Yamada-san ni nani ka iitai desu... sayōnara!
Tom	Yamada-san, konnichiwa. E? Zembu kaitai desu ka.
	Arigatō gozaimasu.
	Uchi no kaisha no e-mail no adoresu o shitteimasu ka.
	Rainen? Hokkaidō ni ikitai desu.
	Edith Palmer-san to issho ni Chotto...
	Sumimasen, sorosoro shuppatsu shimasu.
	Shitsurei shimasu. Sayōnara!

---

* the other day

▶ Spot the keys

Here are two final practice rounds. If you have the recording, close the book now. Find the keywords and try to get the gist of it. Then check on page 90.

1 You might ask a taxi driver:

Kūkō made nanpun gurai desu ka. Ikura desu ka.

His answer:

Sō desu ne. Kōsoku dōro de iku to sanjuppun gurai desu ga kyō wa kōsoku dōro wa kondeiru sō desu. Chotto dame da to omoimasu. Dōro* de ittara ichi jikan gurai kakarimasu ga kondeinai to omoimasu. Kyō wa dōro no hō ga ii desu. Takushī ryōkin desu ka. Dōro de ittara ichimangosen en desu.

*dōro: *road*

2 While killing time in the departure lounge of the airport, you could not help listening to someone who seems to be raving about something. Identify the keywords and guess where they have been.

The answer is on page 90.

...hito wa totemo shinsetsu de minna hansamu desu yo. Soshite o-tenki wa itsumo yokatta desu. Hoteru no shokuji mo yasukute totemo oishikatta desu. Watashitachi wa takusan kankō o shite, totemo kireina tokoro ni ikimashita. Subarashii yasumi deshita kara rainen mata ikitai desu.

Say it simply

1 You are at the airport, about to catch your flight home when you realize that you have left some clothes behind in the room of your hotel. You phone the hotel's housekeeper to ask her to send the things on to you.

2 You are in your own country and you notice a Japanese person looking at a map and looking lost. Can you help them and have a chat with them too?

What would you say? Say it then write it down. Then see page 90.

▶ Let's speak Japanese

Answer these questions using the words in brackets.

1 Tōkyō de apāto o kaimashita ka. (hai, getsuyōbi ni)
2 Hawaii ni ikimashō ka. (hai, kayōbi ni)
3 Akiko-san wa Kate Walker-san ni denwa shimashita ka. (hai, kesa)
4 Dōshite kono kuruma wa supīdo ga demasen ka. (furui, kara)
5 Densha de shuppatsu shimashita ka. (iie, basu)

Ask your Japanese friend very politely to do the following things for you: (use **te kudasaimasen ka**)

6 Help/tell you.
7 Buy an interesting and cheap book.
8 Buy you an English newspaper.
9 Say their phone number for you.
10 Phone your friend.

Now invite your friend to do the following things with you (use **masen ka**)

11 drink beer together in a bar (bā).
12 eat a meal in a restaurant.
13 go to the sports ground and watch football.
14 do some sightseeing in London.
15 go travelling to Hawaii.

Answers

1 Hai, getsuyōbi ni Tōkyō de apāto o kaimashita.
2 Hai kayōbi ni Hawaii ni ikimashō.
3 Hai, Akiko-san wa kesa Kate Walker-san ni denwa shimashita.
4 Kono kuruma wa furui (desu) kara supīdo ga demasen. (Or: Furui (desu) kara kono kuruma wa supīdo ga demasen.)
5 Iie, basu de shuppatsu shimashita.
6 Oshiete kudasaimasen ka.
7 Omoshirokute yasui hon o katte kudasaimasen ka.
8 Eigo no shinbun o katte kudasaimasen ka.
9 O-denwa bangō o itte kudasaimasen ka.
10 Tomodachi ni denwa shite kudasaimasen ka.
11 Bā de bīru o nomimasen ka.
12 Resutoran de shokuji o shimasen ka.
13 Kyōgi jō ni itte, sakkā o mimasen ka.
14 London de kankō shimasen ka.
15 Hawaii ni ryokō shimasen ka.

Let's speak more Japanese

In your own words

This exercise will teach you to express yourself freely. Use only the words you have learned so far.

Tell me in your own words that...

1 next week you have to work
2 you don't like it; you want to go to Hawaii or Fiji
3 your company doesn't know where you are
4 your mother (**haha**) has (knows) the number of your mobile phone
5 Japan is a wonderful country
6 you did a lot of sightseeing and overeating
7 your friend Mr Suzuki is on his way to Osaka today
8 he is catching a train to Hiroshima tomorrow
9 you and your wife must fly (go by plane) to America, because your mother is ill
10 you suggest going to Africa for Christmas, but by boat

Answers

1 Raishū shigoto o shinakereba narimasen.
2 Suki dewa arimasen. Hawaii ka Fiji ni ikitai desu.
3 Watashi ga Nihon ni iru ka kaisha wa shirimasen.
4 Haha wa keitai denwa no denwa-bangō o shirimasu.
5 Nihon wa subarashii kuni desu.
6 Takusan kankō shimashita. Soshite tabesugimashita.
7 Tomodachi no Suzuki-san wa kyō Ōsaka ni ikimasu.
8 Ashita densha de Hiroshima ni ikimasu.
9 Tsuma to hikōki de Amerika ni ikimasu. Haha wa byōki ni narimashita kara.
10 Kurisumasu ni fune de Afurika ni ikimashō.

▶ Let's speak Japanese – fast and fluently

Translate each section and check if it is correct. Then cover the answers and say the three or four sentences fast!

30 seconds for a silver star, 20 seconds for a gold star.

The people in my company (*my colleagues*) do not work a lot.
They write a lot of letters on the computer.
And they always phone their friends.

Watashi no kaisha no hito (watashi no dōryō) *wa amari hataraiteimasen.*
Konpyūta ni tegami o takusan kakimasu.
Soshite itsumo tomodachi ni denwa shimasu.

I know (understand about) Tokyo and Osaka well.
Next year I would like to go to Kyushu.
I didn't buy a book about Japan.

Tōkyō to Ōsaka no koto ga yoku wakarimasu.
Rainen Kyūshū ni ikitai desu.
Nihon no hon o kaimasen deshita.

Hello, why did you come here? What's the matter?
I want to buy a new car and flat. Both (**ryōhō wa**) are very old.
This room is terrible. Can you help me – with 5,000 yen please?

Konnichiwa, dōshite koko ni kimashita ka. Dōshita n desu ka.
Atarashii kuruma to apāto o kaitai desu. Ryōhō wa totemo furui desu.
Kono heya wa hidoi desu. Tetsudatte kudasaimasen ka – gosen-en
de onegaishimasu.

Now say all the sentences in Japanese without stopping and starting. If you can do it in under one minute you are a fast and fluent winner!

But if you are not happy with your result – just try once more.

Test your progress

I have crammed a lot into this last test – nearly all of the **Instant** verbs! But don't panic – it looks worse than it is. Go for it – you'll do brilliantly!

1 We have a computer and so we write a lot of letters.
2 What's the matter? Are you ill? Do you have a headache?
3 We are going with colleagues from the company.
4 We are going to have a meal with friends.
5 The second suitcase is in the bus. Please wait a moment.
6 At Christmas my parents go travelling.
7 What! Someone has eaten my steak!
8 Why didn't you telephone? We waited for three days.
9 Quickly! Call that taxi (over there). We are departing shortly.
10 I have worked on a boat but the salaries are not good.
11 I would like to eat at half past eight. It's not a problem?
12 This restaurant's raw fish is very delicious and it is wonderful.
13 Do you live in a flat in London? (Or) do you live in a house?
14 We have four children. They have already gone to school.
15 My wife always buys too much so I have to work until late.
16 I know Edith Palmer. She always does the shopping with her dog.
17 This place is no smoking? Who said?
18 I want a black T-shirt. Please call the shop assistant.
19 I don't understand (about) computers very well. Please can you help me?
20 They said that your car is very old.
21 What would you like to drink? This red wine is very delicious and not expensive.
22 On Sundays and Mondays the boat leaves at 6.45.
23 We go by plane to Ōsaka. Then we go by car to the apartment.
24 **Instant Japanese** is finished.

Check your answers on page 91. Then enter a final excellent score on the Progress chart and write out your **Certificate**.

Moving on . . .

If you want to continue learning Japanese, try *Teach Yourself Beginner's Japanese*.

answers

How to score

From a total of 100%
- Subtract 1% for each wrong or missing word.
- Subtract 1% for the wrong form of the verb, like **tabemasu** when it should be **tabemashita**.
- Subtract 1% for putting **ni, kara, wa, –kunai, ga, kute** or **no** incorrectly *in front* of the word to which they belong.

There are no penalties for:
- Picking the wrong word where there are two of similar meaning e.g. **ano/are**.
- Wrong word order, as long as **ni, kara, wa, –kunai, ga, kute** or **no** are *after* the word to which they belong.
- Slightly wrong spelling, as long as you say the word! E.g. tsooma (**tsuma**).
- Missing out the odd little word like **o** or **n**, or saying **wa** for **ga** or vice versa.

**100% LESS YOUR PENALTIES WILL GIVE
YOU YOUR WEEKLY SCORE**

Week 1

Test your progress

1 Suzuki-san, hajimemash(i)te.
2 Nihon wa totemo omoshiroi des(u).
3 Ie wa doko des(u) ka/doko ni arimas(u) ka.
4 London ni apāto ga arimas(u).
5 Sannin no kodomo ga imas(u).
6 Rokugatsu ni London wa kirei des(u).

7 Sumimasen, ryokō gaisha wa doko des(u) ka / ni arimas(u) ka.
8 Ginkō ni tomodachi ga imas(u).
9 Mainichi hataraiteimas(u) ka.
10 Itsumo Hong Kong ni ikimas(u).
11 Tsuma wa ichi-gatsu made America de hataraiteimash(i)ta.
12 Hokkaido ni mo ikimash(i)ta.
13 Jun-san no BMW wa dō des(u) ka.
14 Apāto ni ikimas(u) ka.
15 Osoku made hataraiteimas(u). Tsumaranai des(u).

YOUR SCORE: _____ %
Correct your answers. Then read them out loud twice.

Week 2

Test your progress

1 Kōhī o kudasai (or: onegaishimasu).
2 Kono chikaku ni ginkō ga arimasu ka.
3 Sandoicchi, kēki nado mo arimasu.
4 Kōcha wa ikura desu ka.
5 Kono kēki wa amari oishikunai desu.
6 O-shigoto wa nan ji kara desu ka.
7 Itsumo roku ji han ni kissaten ni ikimasu.
8 Toire wa doko desu ka (or: doko ni arimasu ka). Massugu desu ka.
9 Hokkaidō ni ikimasu ka.
10 Shigoto de Tōkyō ni ikimashita.
11 Kono asagohan wa oishii desu. Ikura desu ka.
12 Ashita jū ji han ni doko ni imasu ka.
13 Kurejitto kādo wa tsukaemasen.
14 Ryokō gaisha ni ikimasu. Sorekara Amerika ni ikimasu.
15 Sumimasen, futari dake desu.
16 Ja, sanpaku onegaishimasu.
17 Apāto wa totemo hiroi desu ga chotto takai desu.
18 Kono heya wa warukunai desu ne.
19 Kono amari atsukunai kōcha wa nana hyaku en desu.
20 Kissaten wa koko kara juppun desu.

YOUR SCORE: _____ %

Week 3

Test your progress

1 Kyō wa tenki ga warui desu. Samui desu.
2 Kono chikaku ni ginkō ga arimasu ka.
3 Sumimasen, yūbinkyoku ni ikanakereba narimasen.
4 Kissaten ni ikimashō ka.
5 Ima kara terebi de sakkā ga arimasu ka.
6 Kusuriya wa doko desu ka. Hidarigawa desu ka (or: ni arimasu ka).
7 Ē to... Chotto takakatta desu ga kirei deshō!
8 Ē! Totemo yasukatta desu.
9 Gorufu o mite, shigoto ni ikitai desu.
10 Mōshiwake arimasen ga dorai kurīningu ni ikanakereba narimasen.
11 Ten'in wa hansamu de Brad Pitt ni niteimashita.
12 Ikura deshita ka. Uso!
13 Eigo no shinbun o kaitai desu. O-mise ni ikimashō.
14 Sandoicchi o tabemashita ga kēki wa tabemasen deshita yo.
15 Kinō nani mo kaimasen deshita ga kyō kaisugimashita.
16 Ningyō to yukata o kaimashita.
17 Kitte o kaitai desu.
18 Heya wa chotto semai desu ga daijōbu desu.
19 Kinō terebi de sumō o mimashita ka.
20 Kono kimono wa dame desu. Aoi kimono wa kirei desu.

> **YOUR SCORE: _____ %**

Week 4

Test your progress

1 Mise wa takakute amari yokunai to iimashita.
2 Denwa bangō o/(wa) iimasen deshita.
3 Resutoran wa chotto semai to iimashita.
4 Yasukute ii omiyage-ya o shitteimasu.
5 Ocha wa ikaga desu ka. Soshite gohan wa ikaga desu ka.
6 Kōcha to kōhī to dochira ga ii desu ka.
7 Nan desu ka. Tsukemono wa irimasen ka.
8 Sakana ga daisuki desu. Sashimi ni shimasu.
9 Akai niku wa suki dewa arimasen. Sarada to bīru o onegaishimasu (or: kudasai).
10 Terebi de Sawada Akiko o mimashita. Totemo omoshiroi hito desu.

11 Kaisha kara denwa ga arimashita. Taisetsuna yōji desu.
12 Sumimasen, yakusoku ga arimasu kara jikan ga arimasen.
13 Kinō kare to shokuji o shimashita. Totemo ii kata desu.
14 Isha o yonde kudasai. Byōki ni narimashita.
15 Oshiete kudasai. 'Ice cream' wa, nihongo de nan desu ka.
16 Kenkō no tame ni, o-mizu o nomimasu.
17 Raishū nani o shimasu ka. Shōtengai ni ikitai desu.
18 Kono miso shiru wa suki dewa arimasen. Hidoi desu!
19 Raishū no kayōbi ni Morita-san to issho ni atarashii resutoran ni ikimasu.
20 Osoku made hataraiteimashita. Jūichi ji han ni owarimashita.

```
YOUR SCORE: _____ %
```

Week 5

Test your progress

1 Tōkyō-yuki (or: Tōkyō made) no kippu o san mai kudasai.
2 Kono basu wa suki dewa arimasen. Furusugimasu.
3 Ōfuku (no kippu) wa ikura desu ka.
4 Nan desu ka. Motto yukkuri itte kudasai.
5 Koko wa gakkō desu. Tabako wa dame desu yo.
6 Hayaku, densha ga kimasu. San ban sen desu.
7 Ehagaki o kono posuto ni dashite kudasai. Posuto wa aka(i)desu ka. Sō desu.
8 Kuruma to densha to dochira ga suki desu ka.
9 Gasorin wa tarimasen deshita ga gasorin sutando o mimasen deshita.
10 Asoko ni kusuriya ga arimasu. Basu tei no chikaku desu (or: ni arimasu).
11 Katamichi no kippu o nimai kudasai. Kin'ensha o kudasai (or: onegaishimasu).
12 Itsumo tabako o sutteimasu. Kenkō no tame ni yokunai desu.
13 Kōsoku dōro wa hidoi desu! Densha de ikimasu.
14 Watashi no keitai denwa wa doko desu ka. Keisatsu o yonde kudasai!
15 Ima Igirisu de ame ga futteimasu ga Nihon wa atsusugimasu!
16 Raishū Nihon ni kimasu.
17 Suzuki-san no Toyota Celica ga suki desu. Takakatta desu ka.
18 Ichiban-me no basu wa man'in deshita ga niban-me no wa man'in dewa arimasen deshita.
19 Asoko ni itte kudasai. Basu tei no saki desu. Hidarigawa ni gakkō ga arimasu.

20 Atama ga itai kara nani mo tabemasen deshita!

YOUR SCORE: _____ %

Week 6

Spot the keys

1 On an ordinary road it takes one hour, on the motorway it would be 30 minutes. The fare is 15,000 yen by road.
2 They have of course been to… England!

Say it simply

1 Moshi moshi, Kate Walker desu. Kyō made hoteru ni imashita. Jūni ban no heya deshita. Heya ni wa T.shatsu nado ga arimasu ga ima kūkō ni imasu. Sorosoro shuppatsu shimasu. Igirisu ni dashite kudasai. Watashi no adoresu wa . . . . . . desu. Arigatō gozaimasu.
2 Sumimasen, daijōbu desu ka. Doko ni ikitai desu ka. Koko wa . . . . . . (place name) desu. Aa, ginkō ni ikitai desu ka. Ja, massugu itte, shingō no saki o migi ni magatte kudasai. Koko kara go-hun sugi desu. Wakarimasu ka. Watashi wa . . . . . . (your name) desu. Doko kara desu ka. O-shigoto wa nan desu ka. Doko de hataraiteimasu ka. Sō desu ka. Igirisu ga suki desu ka. Dō desu ka.

Test your progress

1 Konpyūta ga arimasu kara tegami o takusan kakimasu.
2 Dōshita n desu ka. Byōki ni narimashita ka. Atama ga itai desu ka.
3 Kaisha no dōryō to ikimasu.
4 Tomodachi to shokuji o shimasu.
5 Niban-me no sūtsukēsu wa basu no naka ni arimasu. Chotto matte kudasai.
6 Kurisumasu ni ryōshin wa ryokō shimasu.
7 Ē! Dare ka watashi no sutēki o tabemashita!
8 Dōshite denwa shimasen deshita ka. Mikkakan machimashita.
9 Hayaku. Ano takushī o yonde kudasai. Sorosoro shuppatsu shimasu.
10 Fune de hataraiteimashita ga (fune no) kyūryō wa amari yokunai desu.
11 Hachi ji han ni tabetai desu. Daijōbu desu ka.
12 Kono resutoran no sashimi wa totemo oishikute subarashii desu.
13 London de apāto ni sundeimasu ka. Ie ni sundeimasu ka.
14 Yonin no kodomo ga imasu. Mō gakkō ni ikimashita.
15 Tsuma wa itsumo kaisugimasu kara osoku made shigoto o shinakereba narimasen (or: hataraiteimasu).
16 Edith Palmer o shitteimasu. Itsumo inu to kaimono o shimasu.
17 Koko wa kin'en desu ka. Dare ga iimashita ka.
18 Kuroi T. shatsu ga hoshii desu. Ten'in o yonde kudasai.
19 Konpyūta (no koto) wa amari wakarimasen. Oshiete kudasai(masen ka).
20 (Anata no) kuruma wa totemo furui to iimashita.
21 Nomimono wa nani ga yoroshii desu ka. Kono akai wain wa totemo oishikute takakunai desu.
22 Nichiyōbi to getsuyōbi ni fune wa roku ji yonjūgo-hun sugi ni shuppatsu shimasu.
23 Hikōki de Ōsaka ni (or: made) ikimasu. Sorekara kuruma de apāto ni ikimasu.
24 **Instant Japanese** wa owarimashita.

YOUR SCORE: _____ %

how to use the flash cards

The **Flash cards** have been voted the best part of this course! Learning words and sentences can be tedious, but with flash cards it's quick and good fun.

This is what you do:

When the **Day-by-day guide** tells you to use the cards, cut them out. There are 22 **Flash words** and ten **Flash sentences** for each week. Each card has the week number on it, so you won't cut out too many cards at a time or muddle them up later on.

First, try to learn the words and sentences by looking at both sides of the cards. Then, when you have a rough idea, start testing yourself. That's the fun bit. Look at the English, say the Japanese, and then check. Make 'correct', 'wrong' and 'don't know' piles. When all the cards are used up, start again with the 'wrong' pile and try to whittle it down until you get all of them right. You can also play it 'backwards' by starting with the Japanese face up.

Keep the cards in a little box or put an elastic band around them. Take them with you on the bus, the train, to the hairdresser's or the dentist's. If you find the paper too flimsy, photocopy the words and sentences onto card before cutting them up. You could also buy some plain card and stick them on or simply copy them out.

The 22 **Flash words** for each week are there to start you off. Convert the rest of the **New words** to **Flash words,** too. It's well worth it!

> **FLASH CARDS for Instant LEARNING:**
> **DON'T LOSE THEM – USE THEM!**

sumimasen	ikimas(u)
to	ni/de
desu	kara
chotto	ikimash(i)ta
kudasai	hataraite-imas(u)
hajime-mash(i)te	hataraite-imash(i)ta

go, goes [1]	excuse me, sorry [1]
to, at for, from, in [1]	and, with [1]
from [1]	am, is, are [1]
went [1]	a little [1]
work, works, is working [1]	please (may I have) [1]
worked, was/ were working [1]	how do you do? [1]

kaisha [1]	omoshiroi [1]
iie [1]	(ga) arimas(u) [1]
ooi [1]	yasumi [1]
totemo [1]	doko [1]
denwa [1]	kodomo [1]
konnichiwa [2]	shitai [2]

interesting [1]	company [1]
have (own), is [1]	no [1]
holidays [1]	many [1]
where [1]	very [1]
children [1]	telephone [1]
want to do [2]	hello [2]

takakunai [2]	heya [2]
ikura [2]	kurejitto kādo [2]
onegai-shimasu [2]	ii [2]
ashita [2]	asagohan [2]
ikitai desu [2]	kono chikaku ni [2]
kissaten [2]	go-hun sugi [2]

room **2**	not expensive **2**
credit card **2**	how much? **2**
good, nice, all right **2**	please **2**
breakfast **2**	tomorrow **2**
near here **2**	want to go **2**
five minutes past **2**	coffee shop **2**

koko **2**	kōcha **2**
kono **2**	toire **2**
kōhī **2**	massugu **2**
tēburu **2**	sandoicchi **2**
shōtengai **3**	ikimashō **3**
samui **3**	terebi **3**

black tea **2**	this place, here **2**
toilets **2**	this **2**
straight on **2**	coffee **2**
sandwiches **2**	table **2**
let's go **3**	shopping centre **3**
TV **3**	cold **3**

3 yūbinkyoku	**3** kaimasu
3 dake	**3** kusuriya
3 kaitai desu	**3** mise
3 daijōbu	**3** kinō
3 nani mo	**3** watashi no
3 ten'in	**3** de

buy [3]	post office [3]
chemist's [3]	only [3]
shop(s) [3]	want to buy [3]
yesterday [3]	it's OK, no problem [3]
mine [3]	nothing [3]
and [3]	shop assistant [3]

dare _3_	shinbun _3_
kyō _3_	kitte _3_
yasui _3_	kinō _3_
dare ka _4_	denwa bangō _4_
o-kyakusan _4_	yakusoku _4_
moshi moshi _4_	ē/hai _4_

3	3
newspaper	who
3	**3**
stamps	today
3	**3**
yesterday	cheap
4	**4**
phone number	someone
4	**4**
appointment	customer
4	**4**
yes	hello (on phone)

arigatō gozaimasu 4	raishū 4
itsu 4	konban 4
suki dewa arimasen 4	isha 4
sashimi 4	gohan 4
mizu 4	kanjō 4
Igirisu 4	nihongo de 4

4 next week	4 thank you
4 tonight	4 when
4 doctor	4 don't like
4 boiled rice	4 raw fish
4 bill	4 water
4 in Japanese	4 England

4	4
dewa	byōki

4	4
ocha	sutēki

5	5
kippu	katamichi

5	5
ōfuku	tabako

5	5
tsugi	densha

5	5
basu	hito

illness/ill **4**	OK, right **4**
steak **4**	green tea **4**
one way **5**	tickets **5**
cigarettes **5**	return **5**
train **5**	the next **5**
person **5**	bus **5**

posuto 5	hayaku 5
kore 5	sore 5
kuruma 5	are 5
tarimasu 5	atsui 5
keitai denwa 5	ame 5
yukkuri 5	ehagaki 5

quickly **5**	post box **5**
that one **5**	this one **5**
that one over there **5**	car **5**
hot **5**	enough **5**
rain **5**	mobile phone **5**
postcard **5**	slowly **5**

5 tegami	5 keisatsu
6 shinakereba narimasen	6 shirimasen
6 tabun	6 kurisumasu
6 ryokō shimasu	6 fune de
6 mite	6 genki
6 modorimasu	6 subarashii

5 **police**	5 **letter**
6 **don't know**	6 **must do**
6 **Christmas**	6 **perhaps**
6 **by boat**	6 **travel**
6 **healthy, well**	6 **look**
6 **wonderful**	6 **return**

kuni **6**	takusan **6**
kankō **6**	rainen **6**
hon **6**	kyūryō **6**
kite! **6**	sayōnara **6**
kūkō **6**	nani ka **6**
mō **6**	sorosoro **6**

a lot 6	**country** 6
next year 6	**sightseeing** 6
salary 6	**book** 6
goodbye 6	**come on!** 6
something 6	**airport** 6
shortly 6	**already** 6

Smith Peter des(u). [1]

Hiroshima kara des(u) ka. [1]

O-shigoto wa nan des(u) ka. [1]

Honda de hataraiteimas(u). [1]

Ōsaka ni apāto ga arimas(u). [1]

America ni ikimas(u). [1]

London de hataraiteimash(i)ta. [1]

Ginkō wa doko des(u) ka. [1]

Takai des(u). [1]

Ichi-gatsu ni Tōkyō ni imash(i)ta. [1]

I am Peter Smith. [1]

Are you from Hiroshima? [1]

What is your work? [1]

I work at Honda. [1]

I have an apartment in Osaka. [1]

We are going to America. [1]

I was working in London. [1]

Where is the bank? [1]

It is expensive. [1]

I was in Tokyo in January. [1]

Kono chikaku ni kissaten ga arimasu ka. [2]

Hachi ji kara jū ji han made desu. [2]

Shichi ji yonjūgo-hun sugi ni. [2]

Ikura desu ka. [2]

…ni ikitai desu. [2]

Daburu no heya ga arimasu ka. [2]

Asagohan wa nan ji desu ka. [2]

Hidarigawa ni arimasu ka. [2]

Migigawa ni arimasu ka. [2]

Kōhī to sandoicchi o kudasai. [2]

Is there a coffee shop near here? **2**

It is from 8 o'clock to half past 10. **2**

At a quarter to eight. **2**

How much is it? **2**

We would like to go to… **2**

Do you have a double room? **2**

At what time is breakfast? **2**

Is it on the left side? **2**

Is it on the right side? **2**

May I have a coffee and a sandwich please? **2**

Mōshiwake arimasen ga... 3

Kaimono o shimashō. 3

...ni ikanakereba narimasen. 3

...ni ikimashō ka. 3

Nan ji made desu ka. 3

Daijōbu desu. 3

Chotto takakatta desu. 3

Nani ga arimasu ka. 3

Nani mo kaimasen deshita. 3

Eigo no shinbun o kaitai desu. 3

I am sorry but… **3**

Let's do some shopping. **3**

I/we must go to… **3**

Shall we go to…? **3**

Until what time? **3**

No problem/It's OK. **3**

It was a bit expensive. **3**

What is there? **3**

I didn't buy anything. **3**

I want to buy an
English newspaper. **3**

Totemo ii kata desu. 4

Taisetsuna yōji desu. 4

Sutēki to sarada ni shimasu. 4

Shitsurei shimasu. 4

Kōhī wa suki dewa arimasen. 4

Oshiete kudasai. 4

...wa nihongo de nan desu ka. 4

Isha o yonde kudasai. 4

...wa ikaga desu ka. 4

Nani ga yoroshii desu ka. 4

He/She is a very nice person. **4**

It is an important matter. **4**

I will go for steak and salad. **4**

Sorry for disturbing you. **4**

I don't like coffee. **4**

Can you help/tell me, please? **4**

How do you say … in Japanese? **4**

Please call the doctor. **4**

How about/would you like…? **4**

What would you like? **4**

Katamichi no kippu o
nimai kudasai. 5

Sumimasen, motto
yukkuri itte kudasai. 5

Tsugi no densha wa
nan ji desu ka. 5

Nan ban sen desu ka. 5

Kono basu wa
shōtengai made desu ka. 5

Kōsoku dōro wa doko
desu ka. 5

Migigawa ni gasorin
sutando ga arimasu. 5

Dōshite kaimashita ka.
Suki deshita kara! 5

Ichiban-me no wa
takasugimashita. 5

Atama ga itai desu. 5

Two single tickets please. 5

Excuse me, can you 5
speak more slowly?

What time is the next train? 5

What number platform 5
is it?

Does this bus go to the 5
shopping area?

Where is the motorway? 5

There is a petrol station 5
on the right.

Why did you buy it? 5
Because I liked it!

The first one was too 5
expensive.

I have a headache. 5

O-genki desu ka. 6

O-yasumi wa dō 6
deshita ka.

Issho ni bīru o 6
nomimasen ka.

Nihon ni itta koto ga 6
arimasen.

Shigoto o shinakereba 6
narimasen.

Dōshita n desu ka. 6

Chotto matte kudasai. 6

Yoku tegami o kakimasu. 6

Kono aida wa 6
arigatō gozaimashita.

Nihon wa subarashii 6
kuni desu.

How are you? 6

How were your holidays? 6

Would you like a beer with me? 6

I have never been to Japan. 6

I have to work. 6

What's the matter? 6

Please wait a moment. 6

I write letters often. 6

Thank you for the other day. 6

Japan is a wonderful country. 6

*This is to certify
that*

....

*has successfully completed
a six-week course of*

Instant Japanese

with .... *results*

Date   *Instructor*